Shabih Zaidi
Globally Mobile Intellectual Capital:
Narratives of Corporate Executives & Families on the Move

Shabih Zaidi

GLOBALLY MOBILE
INTELLECTUAL CAPITAL

Narratives of Corporate Executives & Families on the Move

Bibliografische Information der Deutschen Nationalbibliothek
Die Deutsche Nationalbibliothek verzeichnet diese Publikation in der Deutschen Nationalbibliografie; detaillierte bibliografische Daten sind im Internet über http://dnb.d-nb.de abrufbar.

Bibliographic information published by the Deutsche Nationalbibliothek
Die Deutsche Nationalbibliothek lists this publication in the Deutsche Nationalbibliografie; detailed bibliographic data are available in the Internet at http://dnb.d-nb.de.

Cover painting by Shabih Zaidi, 2016

ISBN-13: 978-3-8382-1652-2
© *ibidem*-Verlag, Stuttgart 2022
Alle Rechte vorbehalten

Das Werk einschließlich aller seiner Teile ist urheberrechtlich geschützt. Jede Verwertung außerhalb der engen Grenzen des Urheberrechtsgesetzes ist ohne Zustimmung des Verlages unzulässig und strafbar. Dies gilt insbesondere für Vervielfältigungen, Übersetzungen, Mikroverfilmungen und elektronische Speicherformen sowie die Einspeicherung und Verarbeitung in elektronischen Systemen.

All rights reserved. No part of this publication may be reproduced, stored in or introduced into a retrieval system, or transmitted, in any form, or by any means (electronical, mechanical, photocopying, recording or otherwise) without the prior written permission of the publisher. Any person who does any unauthorized act in relation to this publication may be liable to criminal prosecution and civil claims for damages.

Printed in the EU

Abstract

The concentration of pharmaceutical research and production in Basel is unique and the influx of highly skilled professionals and their families has changed the local landscape over the past few decades. This thesis is based on ethnographic research carried out in Basel between 2016 and 2019. The experiences of families moving to work in Basel on an International Assignment is explored through the lens of Corporate Mobility from the company's perspective. I also wanted to understand how the move was experienced by the family accompanying the Corporate Executive. Interviews with both the employee and the spouse allowed me to explore their various motivating factors and also acknowledge the unique aspects of life in Basel.

Using Grounded Theory to analyse my semi-structured interviews, I argue that emotions play a strong role in both the professional and personal spheres. I started with Human Resources (HR) literature, explored studies of the migration of the 'highly skilled' and used my Coaching & Training development knowledge to inform this dissertation with a multiple perspectives approach. I chose not to focus on ethnicity, gender or nationality during my fieldwork, but tried to gain as much as possible through personal discussions, participant observation and full immersion in the field whilst collating numerous biographical accounts.

Globally Mobile Intellectual Capital is critical to companies and starts with the individual's self-realisation when entering the corporate world. Leveraging this concept and negotiating the career-plus-personal trajectory of the individual and their family are key to understanding the benefits and also some of the challenges that mobility offers.

I use Sensorialscapes to highlight the flow of emotions as embodied and practised by mobile individuals connecting to a space via the senses.

Profiles

Chris & Anne, American, mid-50s, came to Basel on a 3-year contract and left behind their two college-aged sons in the US. They decided to bring no furniture with them and moved into a flat on the Rhine. This is their first move abroad.

Patrick & Mary, Irish, late 40s, here on their second stint in Basel with three teenage children, all at the International School. They moved from Ireland to Basel 10 years ago, then moved to the UK and are back in Basel again.

Carlos, Spanish, mid-30s, single. Moved to Basel 6 months before I interviewed him. This is his first move abroad.

Stefanie & Thomas, German, late 40s, 2 teenage children at the Swiss International School. In Basel for 2 years after other international assignments away from their base in Germany, including France and Singapore.

Rajesh & Jaya, Indian, mid-40s, 1 son. Moved to Basel from Thailand 10 months before I spoke to them and just accepted another international assignment to Turkey. This is their 7th year abroad.

Lucy & Axel, British-American, mid-40s, two children in primary school. Lucy was brought up 'on the move' and this is the family's second time in Switzerland. Her American husband had not moved prior to their first stint 6 years ago.

Helle, German, single, early 50s. Located in Basel now after living in the US for a decade. Went to the US on an assignment and then moved to Basel initially for a short period but then decided to stay.

Robert & Shauna, American, late 40s, two teenagers at the International school. Five years into their first assignment abroad. Moving back to another city in the US.

Carmen & Chloe, American, mid 40s, first assignment abroad. Two middle school children at the International school. They are moving back to the US after this assignment.

Table of Contents

Abstract 5
Profiles 6
Table of Contents 8
Chapter 1 : Introduction 11
    i. Research Question / Collection of Biographies 13
    ii. The Field and Biographical sample 15
    iii. Methodology: interviews, participant observation 16
    iv. Observing Oneself: Positionality 18
    v. Defining Corporate Mobility and Fieldwork 21
    vi. Mobility Factors 23
    vii. Framework 23

Chapter 2 : Plug In / Plug Out 27
    i. Working Strategies 28
    ii. Working together 29
    iii. On the Personal Front 31
    iv. Affective Analysis 33
    v. Containing Perspectives 35
    vi. Conclusion 36

Chapter 3 : Families on the Move 37
    i. Mobility Snapshots 39
    ii. Conclusion 47

Chapter 4 : Intellectual Capital as Currency 49
    i. Language as Currency 52
    Conclusion 54

Chapter 5 : Mobility Flows: Emotions; Food, Rituals, Memory. 57
    i. Affect Theory Unpacked 59
    ii. Sensorial Mobility 60

iii. Emotional Capital 62
iv. Emotions on the Move 65
v. Conclusion 66

Chapter 6 : Transnational Transformations 69
i. Management Matters 69
ii. Mobile Leaders 73
iii. Success Factors 75
iv. Conclusion 77

Chapter 7 : Basel Topography & Features 79
i. Imaginary of Basel 80
ii. (Un)common Spaces 81
iii. Conclusion 88

Chapter 8: Basel is Unique – City Life 91
i . Reality Bites 94
ii. International School Bubble 97
iii. (In)Visible Boundaries 99
iv. Consuming Cosmopolitanism 101
v. Conclusion 102

Chapter 9: Mobility or Not? 103
i. Dual Career Choices 105
ii. Support Networks 106
iii. Conclusion 109

Chapter 10 : Swiss Spaces 111
i. Gruezi! Greetings! 111
ii. Permission, Please! 113
iii. Integration Means? 115
iv. Conclusion 117

Chapter 11: Exploring 'I' 119
    i. Getting to know Basel 121
    ii. Learning By Doing 123
    iii. University Experience 124
    iv. What does this mean? 127
    v. Conclusion 128

Chapter 12 : Sensorialscapes 129
    i. Linking Spatialities 129
    ii. Emotional Capital 130
    iii. Discomfort Explored 131
    iv. Conclusion 132

Chapter 13. Concluding Findings and Remarks 133
    1. Mobility enhances career and personal trajectories .. 133
    2. Intellectual Capital leads to Mobility and Mobility leads to Intellectual Capital 134
    3. Emotional Capital Accumulation 134
    4. Agency 135
    5. Culture & Belonging 135
    6. Loose Ends 136
    i. Complexity of Success 137
    ii. Mobility & Identity Markers 138
    iii. Globalisation, Self & Ethnography 138
    iv. PhD 2015 — Pandemic 2020 139

References 141
Acknowledgements 151

Chapter 1 : Introduction

> 'We've come here as expats on assignment and want to explore Europe as much as possible. My husband has a lot of stress at work, so we try to take as many short breaks nearby to enjoy the experience of living here.'
>
> Ann, Spouse

Switzerland, like other OECD (Organisation for Economic Co-operation and Development) countries, depends on a considerable number of 'foreign' workers. Since this thesis is focused on the 'highly skilled' workforce employed by pharmaceutical companies in Basel, I include below a table that highlights the importance of the Chemical and Pharmaceutical Industries to the Swiss economy.

Figure 1. Top ten Swiss chemical and pharmaceutical companies in 2012.		
Company	Revenue	Employees
Novartis	$59.5 billion	130,000
Roche	$51.0 billion	82,000
Syngenta	$15.1 billion	27,000
Clariant	$8.7 billion	21,000
Sika	$5.4 billion	15,000
Givaudan	$4.7 billion	9,000
Omya	$4.7 billion	6,000
Lonza	$4.4 billion	11,000
Galencia	$3.7 billion	7,000
Firmenich	$2.9 billion	6,000

HandelsZeitung, 'Switzerland's Top-Ten Chemical Companies, 2012', www.handelszeitung.ch (June 27, 2013).

Many of these companies are headquartered in Basel and this fact alone indicates the diverse nature of the city and the attraction of Switzerland as a favourable working destination for mobile individuals and families. The country spends a considerable amount of time and resources on branding itself, promoting its low taxes, good salaries, impeccable environment and high standard of living.

The migration of a highly qualified workforce to Switzerland is a topic that has been studied through different lenses at many local institutions including the University of Basel.[1] These projects focus on learning more about the lived experience of the migrant population availing itself of numerous strategies to live and work in Switzerland. Again, since my focus is limited to a specific group, Company Executives and their families, I am only trying to present the larger framework within which my fieldsite is situated. I am not dealing with the 'highly skilled' per se but with a category within the highly skilled, that of Corporate Management Leaders. The general political as well as local and national economic ramifications of migratory processes are not covered in this study. The Swiss National Science Foundation (SNSF) supports research projects through funding initiatives that promote research excellence in accordance with its mission statement 'Knowledge is the Key to the Future: Research Creates Knowledge' (www.snf.ch). The Swiss government fully supports the impetus for a knowledge-based economy at all levels . This plays a role in the number of highly qualified foreigners living in Basel, which by some accounts amounts to approximately 30% of the resident population.

---

[1] At the Institute of Cultural Anthropology and European Ethnology at the University of Basel, a number of research projects funded by the Swiss National Science Foundation (SNSF) were underway when I joined and discussions with colleagues helped me to define my own focus. 'The Mobility of the Highly Skilled Towards Switzerland' by Prof. Walter Leimgruber, Dr Metka Hercog and Dr Laure Sandoz; 'Narratives of Identity, Multi-sited Biographies and Transnational Life-modes of Highly Qualified Migrants: Two Case Studies' by Prof. Jacques Picard, Helene Oberle and Haddy Sarr; 'Movements of Entrepreneurs of Born Global Startups' by Dr Katrin Sontag; and 'Swiss Living Abroad' by Dr Aldina Camenisch & Seraina Mueller have all informed my research through collegial discussions.

Basel is located on the Rhine river, which divides the city into two parts: Basel City and Basel Land. This division has political implications since the two parts compose two separate states (Cantons) of the 26 that make up the Swiss Federation. The Swiss Cantons, like the states in the US, have their own unique identity, history, traditions and even public holidays. Cantons send representatives to the Swiss Parliament and, importantly for foreign workers, are in charge of issuing relevant work permits. The borders with France and Germany are approximately 15 minutes from the centre of Basel, the third largest city in Switzerland after Zürich and Geneva. The official language is German although a dialect (Basel Deutsch) is spoken locally.

As noted in the above table, there are a cluster of chemical and pharmaceutical companies in Basel and these make it punch above its weight economically in the region. Transport connectivity is excellent, with trams, buses and trains running smoothly, along with plenty of flights servicing the EuroAirport. I will outline more details regarding the topography of Basel in a later chapter to further underline its uniqueness.

i. Research Question / Collection of Biographies

How is mobility experienced by Corporate Executives and their families? This question is the starting point for my biographical thesis that Globally Mobile Intellectual Capital constitutes a form of currency that creates new opportunities for those involved: executives and their families, and of course the companies that facilitate their move. The participants in my study are often viewed as a privileged elite living within their own social 'bubble'.

Locating my fieldwork in Basel, I have focused on the Pharmaceutical Industry because Novartis and Roche, along with several other important supporting industry players, have their headquarters here. This rich offering of multinational companies has created a vibrant self-described 'expatriate' population that is transient in nature. I use the word 'expatriate' generically to refer to my field informants, Corporate Executives who have moved here with their families for a limited number of years. There are many other members of the local population who also refer to themselves as 'expatriates', since they are not living in their country of origin, but they are not part of this study. I will go deeper into the labelling of categories in the course of this dissertation.

What does it take to settle into a new job at the Basel headquarters and how do the families adjust to their new environment? What factors contribute to a successful relocation? Are there certain mechanisms that can be used to construct 'home' and what does that mean to these families? How is belonging negotiated on a daily basis to create a familiar rhythm?

I have used Grounded Theory to probe my data in the larger framework of migration studies vis-à-vis, to start with, the concepts of Globalization and Mobility. What I quickly discovered in my interviews was the emotionally charged nature of the experience. That led me to explore the importance of the senses as a means of locating, creating and grounding oneself in a particular space. My colleague Marta Rudnicka (PhD Candidate in Social Anthropology) and I explored this concept at length with our students in a course that we developed and taught at the University of Basel called Anthropological Perspectives on Sensorial Mobility.

Using Affect Theory as a framework to examine and articulate subjective and intersubjective states (Svašek 2014), we explored the literature on the senses, migration studies and globalization to delve into key aspects of human behaviour. I use the concept of *Sensorialscapes* to designate the idea of connecting to a place through the senses in order to create a familiar rhythm that would provide a level of comfort and a feeling of being settled. Those individuals who were successful at negotiating *Sensorialscapes* for themselves, thus establishing a comfortable connection to Basel, reported high levels of satisfaction with their lives.

The research design included multiple interviews with Corporate Executives and their spouses to probe the many aspects of the process of their relocation to Basel. I have anonymised the accounts; however, several familiar tropes can be recognized as typical experiences of newcomers to Basel. The collection of biographies below highlights the many conversations I have had about the migration experiences of this group. These narratives allow a deeper exploration of what it means to move.

ii. The Field and Biographical sample

Being in Basel, it is hard to ignore the impact of the Pharmaceutical Industry on the local economy, population and architecture. My office at the University of Basel is at Rheinsprung 9/11 and I can see the Roche Tower to my right and the Novartis campus to my left. The question that a non-Swiss person living in Basel is most commonly asked first is 'do you work at Novartis or Roche?' There are very few people who do not have some sort of link to either company or a related industry. I was intrigued by the experience of individuals who moved here for work and brought their families to this unique part of the world. Companies spend a lot of money, time and resources on Talent Management, supporting executives and their families to ensure that relocations are smooth. I was curious to learn the narratives of these individual and the meaning they gave to this experience. How did it affect them on an individual, family and career level? Could the findings of this study be used to better inform companies and individuals of the ramifications this kind of lifestyle choice has? Why were some moves more successful than others and what could be done for a more positive outcome?

These were some of the questions I wanted to explore when I started and, in a sense, they mirrored my own experience of moving with my family to different locations. I knew what corporate mobility meant for us and wanted to explore if there were ways of better understanding the processes involved in order to facilitate positive outcomes for individuals, families and companies. As a Coach it quickly became apparent to me that this area required more attention, vital as it is for companies' Organisation Development, for Leadership qualities in Executives and, critically, for the Mindset of individuals and their families. In effect, these all intersect at the individual level where I use Emotions as an analytical tool to delve deeper into what the key indicators for success are.

iii. Methodology: interviews, participant observation

The question of who is considered a globally mobile executive is highly problematic and subject to many different factors. With that in mind, the biographical data collected for this study was in the form of semi-structured one-on-one interviews with an executive and their spouse, on a mobile career trajectory determined by their company or driven by themselves. The sample is reflective of the multinational makeup of the companies and is not categorised according to gender, nationality, age or ethnicity unless a strong trend emerges from the data.

In addition, I sought to explore mobility through self-descriptive words such as 'mobile', 'expat', 'lucky" and 'lifestyle', used by some of my informants in casual conversations which fortunately led to interviews. This group of migrants are highly skilled and sought-after individuals, occupying a 'bubble' on the fringes of society and building up cultural capital (Bourdieu 1986) as they move from country to country. Their transnational lives often transcend borders, ethnicities, genders and the resultant effect is that of a certain 'malleability' which allows them to mingle with other globally mobile individuals. There is a lot of literature that explores the experience of such families and my research intention was to explore the meaning of the lived experience in Basel particularly.

Whilst the duration of their stay is a factor, as many fixed short-term contract employees may not invest as much into their new surroundings, the overall majority of employees, along with their families, go through a varying number of issues when trying to settle into their new home. They need to 'integrate' not only into the mainstream Swiss community, but also into Basel's large international community, all the while trying to maintain a sense of family identity.

The detailed biographies collected necessitated an individual-level analysis of the narratives and meanings produced as a result of mobility. I started by using Grounded Theory (Glaser & Strauss 1967) with the additional developments of Corbin (1998) and Charmaz (1998). Analysis of the data to determine the social networks maintained and created and what these established for the informant helped in understanding the adjustment process. Biographies are powerful narratives that link memories, places, spaces, objects and people through storytelling and, I would venture, the concept of *Sensorialscapes*. By marking out and connecting key life events as a 'journey', by using language that is often evocative, the Narrator conveys emotions that are central to the process of communicating hopes, dreams, motivations, etc., moments that are (de)constructed with a touch of self-reflection and nostalgia. Using biographies as a way to approach and understand an informant's perspective on their own life trajectories 'means new interpretations of the past and new meanings, sometimes even reinterpretations in the light of current or recent events or evaluations can be woven into older layers of the experience … People and their life stories appear in dynamic relationships whose interaction involves different and interdependent vectors: people, groups, times, spaces, things, symbols, ideas, dreams, properties, institutions, actions and movements' (Picard 2016; my translation)

Collecting these biographies as data for my research was an exercise in active listening and open questioning. This allowed 'the understanding of a perspective of both subjective and individual experiences, as well as of structural or institutional areas considered to be methodologically equivalent by actors. The concepts of biography and the lived environment can help draw out insights from interviews and participant observation about a complex narrative that condenses the situation' (Picard 2016; my translation).

The semi-structured interviews were conducted individually with a view to establishing an open and confidential conversation about the decision to move to Basel and how they dealt with the whole relocation process, starting from logistical matters to the settling-in phase and to their current situation. As a member of the international community it was easy to establish a rapport with my informants and I was mindful of not leading the conversation, but just listening and waiting for thoughts to develop and explanations to be expanded upon.

iv. Observing Oneself: Positionality

As an ethnographer, the concept of positionality truly hit home for me on multiple levels whilst writing and reflecting upon this topic. It is no longer the simple binary of 'Insider/Outsider', originally developed in the field of anthropology when the early anthropologists travelled to distant lands in search of 'untouched cultures', which could be studied through the lens of 'the Other'. Nowadays we can look at our computer screens and explore 'new tribes' and 'new spaces' at any moment. The description or understanding of culture as 'shared webs of meaning' (Geertz 1973) has become synonymous with talking about the collective human experience of a system. How can we describe and understand the meaning of a lived experience through the everyday connections human beings make with their environment? What are the limitations and possibilities of this kind of ethnographic study, and is there ever a moment when we, as researchers, can truly capture through analysis what is fully meant by 'thick description'?(Geertz 1973).

When I started this dissertation, I was trying to grasp what mobility meant to the families that experienced several global relocations through work. Would there be an 'aha' moment for me that would enable me to shed more light on the countless studies that have been conducted to understand the impact of such a lifestyle? Looking at the HR literature it became obvious that this topic is of extreme importance to companies since they spend millions of dollars supporting corporate relocation. Strategies and programmes to retain and support top executives are part of HR policies looking to adopt a more holistic approach when dealing with international recruitment, providing realistic information about the social context of living conditions, a paramount consideration for families. Cross-cultural adjustment is linked to positive career outcomes such as career satisfaction, life satisfaction and intention to stay (Guo & Al Ariss 2105). In her talk at a class led by Dr Metka Hercog, Thusanthy Sinniah from the University of Applied Sciences and Arts Northwestern Switzerland (FHNW) School of Business highlighted some multinational company practices seeking to confront the challenges of International Assignments. Socio-cultural factors play an important role in adjustment and, according to Sinniah, there is a growing trend for Cultural Awareness seminars. This is something that I too have noticed in my Coaching practice.

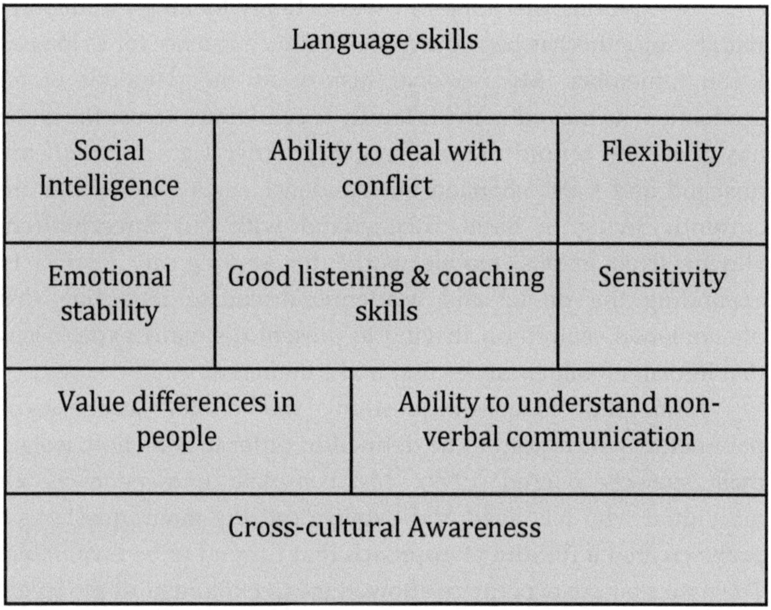

Language skills		
Social Intelligence	Ability to deal with conflict	Flexibility
Emotional stability	Good listening & coaching skills	Sensitivity
Value differences in people	Ability to understand non-verbal communication	
Cross-cultural Awareness		

Figure 2. Socio-cultural competencies, Thusanthy Sinniah 2015

As Switzerland is highly selective about issuing work permits and as companies also constantly review and revise their Talent Management policies in order to remain globally competitive (https://hbr.org/2018/03/the-new-rules-of-talent-management), the practices adopted by the local pharmaceutical giants grew more interesting. I had many questions at the outset. How can the success of relocation be measured so that companies can ensure a return on investment? What factors contribute to the failure of these moves and can these situations be mitigated in order to facilitate a smooth transition? 'While the traditional expatriation of HQ personnel to foreign subsidiaries continues to serve as a prominent and useful global staffing strategy, global organizations are simultaneously diversifying their pool of global employees (Mayrhofer, Reichel, &

Sparrow 2012) to meet the demands driven by the globalization of business. The mix of international assignment methods, beyond expatriation or home-country nationals, is felt with an increasing presence of host or third-country nationals at HQ locations (GMAC, 2014)' (http://dx.doi.org/10.1080/09585192.2015.1052086).

By exploring this subject, I was actually looking for answers within, since this has been the context of my existence for as long as I can remember. My personal history as the daughter of an academic who moved with his family several times across the globe has given me a fluid view of mobility. After I got married, my husband and I also changed our residence several times and are currently living in Basel, Switzerland with our three children. Having lived in this 'mobile world' for so long, my interest in expanding the public and academic discourse regarding this phenomenon centred on striving to present the many experiences that inform mobile lifestyles and make them real.

Ethnographers face the question of methodology as a series of parameters which need to be defined in order to somehow isolate their subjects (Herod 1999). My complete immersion as an individual who has lived and experienced the many questions I probe created a fluidity of approach that I found to be invaluable. The nature of my experience allowed me to explore multiple levels and perspectives, whilst questioning my own assumptions at every turn. Who is able to gain more depth in a subject, an insider or outsider? For me, the many blurred lines only led to a better understanding of the myriad aspects of my subjects' lived experience. I therefore define my positionality as an auto-ethnographer seeking to 'research that [which] involves self-observation and reflexive investigation in the context of ethnographic field work and writing' (Marechal 2010: 43).

My recognition of underlying assumptions based on personal experience and own history is very strong and I have used it to further develop and question my material through probing my informants, sometimes matching their ideas and at other times opposing and questioning the reasoning underlying emerging themes. This circularity of approach allows for the expression of the complexity lived and experienced by my informants. After all, is it ever possible to determine the exact cause and effect of life strategies given that they are often quite particular? Allowing such a broad spectrum of analysis at the beginning, however, is problematic in that there seems to be no focal point around which to centre the discussion. To address this, I wish to provide a flexible framework that can be used to determine the major perspectives, motivations and experiences of this kind of lifestyle so that companies and individuals are better informed when thinking about International Assignments.

v. Defining Corporate Mobility and Fieldwork

The global mobility of Corporate Executives and their families, and the issue of maintaining relationships as a result of relocation, may be regarded as a private matter. However, the impact on employee performance as a result of poor family adjustment to a new environment cannot be overestimated. Social networks need to be constantly reinforced and maintained in order to preserve ties with friends and relatives who live far away. Many issues crop up as a result of the 'hard work' involved in the task of 'keeping in close touch' and the realisation that social relations are affected. The 'emotional labour' involved in international mobility (Yeoh et al 2005) exemplifies how emotions play a major role in the complexity of mobile family life. Judgements vary as to whether or not irregular contact with other family members and friends is destructive of relationships and intimacy. Is it the rule that the fewer ties you have, and the weaker that they are, the easier it is to be mobile (Nowicka, 2005)?

Much research has been done to understand the adjustment process of families, particularly the accompanying spouse, in order to inform company HR policies and it is a growing field in the social sciences (Ackers 2005). In my research, viewing it through the analytical lens of mobility allows further exploration of the observable practices, imaginaries and experience of relocation on the lives of those who have chosen to move to Basel and make it their 'home'. Global Mobility is an essential component of a company's success (KPMG [2013]: International Assignment

Policies and Practices of Swiss Headquartered Companies), which is why understanding how to manage and possibly increase the chances of a smooth transition for mobile families is important. Although much is on offer already, and the company provides a lot of support, the narratives collected in my research point to varying degrees of 'settlement'.

As such, I focus on Corporate Executives who are highly skilled Management Leaders and work for the Pharmaceutical Industry, based in Basel, and their families. My connections with this group are through the International School of Basel where many Executives send their children and where my own children go to school. I have also had the opportunity, as a Professional Coach and Trainer, to conduct soft skills workshops on Personal Effectiveness to employees in various locations in Europe, and offered Coaching on an individual basis. This has allowed me to fully capture and experience the working environment conveyed by my interviewees and also in my own capacity as an external Associate Trainer.

These multiple layers of connections allowed me to build an easy rapport with my interviewees that often led to shared stories and greater understanding of the unique environment that our lifestyles create. The question of privilege often comes up within this circle and it is acknowledged as the result of 'many years of hard work' which can now be enjoyed, albeit only temporarily because the next assignment is looming, often after an average of a 3-year stay in one location. Of course there is also a 'price to pay' for this life: leaving family, familiar surroundings, friends, work … a sometimes exhausting list which tempers the feeling of exclusivity. The phrase 'first-world problems' is jokingly used to minimise feelings of discomfort and despair. The settling-in process can be difficult, yet the overarching idea of privilege can make it even more emotionally complicated by raising opposing feelings: *'we are so lucky to be able to experience this lifestyle, so why is this so difficult and why does the inability to speak the local language make me cry?'* (Ann).

vi. Mobility Factors

Whilst conducting my research, I have been fortunate enough to determine some of the motivating factors that went into the decision making process. The variables differ considerably from family to family but some of the major factors that resulted in the move to Basel are: career growth, adventure, international exposure for the children, a better lifestyle, more opportunities. I will unpack the various links which became clear in my data analysis, such as the effect of relocation on career trajectories for the working spouse but also for the stay-at-home spouse, how the age of the children impacts the decision, whether local language is a factor, etc. Some of the difficulties are common regardless of location but there are some that seem to be specific to Basel. The fact that Novartis and Roche have their Global Headquarters in Basel means that the top tier of Corporate Executives reside here at some point in their career. The various aspects of relocating to Basel, taking into account its topographical features, which I outline in Chapter 7, is what I have tried to capture through the many interviews and mark out what is important about this study.

The main approach at the outset was to allow the informants to describe their migration process as a fluid narrative in order to allow various perspectives and motivations to come to the fore. This allowed for loose connections around arrival, settling-in, school, work, daily life, language to emerge. By looking at how individuals constructed their stories, I was able to discern patterns that enabled understanding how they made sense of their move(s) and negotiated their everyday lives in Basel.

vii. Framework

In the following chapters, I present my field research as, using Grounded Theory (Strauss & Corbin 1999), I started to collect data and observations which I could analyse and probe with theories and questions that teased out the meaning of corporate mobility. Through peer discussions, literature reviews and participant observation, I was led to the emotions and the relational nature through which, once understood, they can be used to add 'thick description' (Geertz 1973) to practices and corporate settings, and be leveraged to enhance leadership skills. This work synthesises the concepts of Migration, Globalisation, Mobility and Transnationalism through the emotions as *cultural vessels*. Movement and flows across boundaries (re)produce transnational social fields through everyday practices. 'Increasingly emotions are recognised not as individualised, internal psychological states but as fundamentally intersubjective and thus social and cultural in character' (Ahmed 2004 b: 9; Svašek and Skrbis 2007: 371). 'It has been argued that the more rapid pace of internationalization and globalization leads to a more strategic role for HumanResource Management' (HRM) (Novicevic & Harvey 2001; Scullion& Starkey 2000). 'In particular, a shortage of leadership talent is a major obstacle many companies face as they seek to operate on a global scale. The rhetoric of maximizing the talent of individual employees as a unique source of competitive advantage has been a central element of strategic HR policy in recent years' (Frank & Taylor 2004; Lewis & Heckman 2006). By moving beyond what is often seen as a transactional arrangement between companies and their mobile talent, I hope to provide further insights into the lived experience of mobile Corporate Executives and their families.

The chapters are organised into three main parts:

Introduction:

Chapter 1:   Describes the fieldsite, my reasoning for pursuing this research and the context of this study

Chapter 2:   Details the experience of the working spouse, stay-at-home spouse/family as they transition to Basel

Chapter 3:   Profiles of some of the informants who participated in semi-structured interviews

Discussion and Analysis:

Chapter 4: Mobility and Leadership as practised and experienced by individuals and companies

Chapter 5: Uses of Globalisation Flows and Affect Theory to introduce my analytical contribution of emotions captured in *Sensorialscapes*

Chapter 6: What success looks like as a Leader; the valued skills and traits

Chapter 7: Grounding my study in Basel highlights some of the factors that contribute and hinder placemaking (topography)

Chapter 8: Looking at support networks

Chapter 9: A Swiss institution that supports government policy

Chapter 10: *Sensorialscapes* as an analytical tool

Conclusion:

Chapter 11: Synthesis of the material

Chapter 12 : Summary and final conclusion

Chapter 2 : Plug In / Plug Out

The idea of moving to a different environment and setting up from scratch is a daunting prospect. The stories related to the physical packing up and moving are just as important as the emotional connections that one loses, makes or changes in the process. All the myriad elements that make up this process, both the positives and the negatives, inform the series of adjustments required before one can say that one feels 'settled'. Even after making such a declaration, one is often in a tenuous state which can be affected by a change in personal or professional circumstances and this can lead to feelings of instability. The nature of this lifestyle is such that there is always an element of uncertainty around how long this 'settled state' will last before it is affected by an external factor such as a job change, or a friend moving away, or economic uncertainty, or emotional distress due to a family crisis ... The list is potentially endless and it is important to be able to find a way to establish oneself in what can be an uncertain, temporary situation. I asked my interviewees how they found ways to adapt to this situation. In what ways did they plug into a location and then plug out?

In this chapter, I start by looking at how the arrival process unfolds for both spouses in their respective environments, with the aim of getting a better understanding of the emotional connections left behind and the new ones made as they transition. 'Transnational migrants characteristically participate in an array of activities — mediated by flows of material objects and symbolic ties — to reproduce their transnational social fields ... [There are] affective and emotional dimensions ... of what motivates, compels and structures transnational actors' participation across borders' (Wise & Velayutham 2017) (https://doi.org/10.1080/00207659.2017.1300468). Probing the emotional dimension of the migration narrative proved to be the key starting point for my analysis.

i. Working Strategies

For the working spouse, the familiarity of the corporate work environment means that the rhythm of their workday experience is quite similar from place to place, particularly if they are in the same company. The patterns of a new job may mean new colleagues or more/less travel or a new area of expertise but the stretch is taken as a professional challenge, one with a support network of colleagues and processes to facilitate success in place. The executives are provided with benchmarks with which to familiarise themselves and performance measures to indicate how successful they are at achieving targets and ticking off required work-related goals and objectives.

> 'Working here is not that different than how it would be anywhere else, I mean I am in HR and so it is always a bit frustrating at the beginning because you don't know all the people … I was kind of starting fresh but quickly started building my network to do my job more effectively.'
>
> Lucy, Executive

The multinational working environment, with English as the business language of use, allows for a smooth transfer of skills and built-up knowledge capital, both of which can be utilised from the moment of arrival. The main challenges stated were adapting to the relational change in people and networks, understanding the organisational set up and how to negotiate with multiple stakeholders.

> 'The one thing I was coached to do before coming over here was to please listen and do not start talking fast like Americans usually do! I listened and discovered that I could start picking up the nuances of the conversations with my colleagues, even with Brits I had to train my ear to the many accents. Everybody is speaking English but now I am more adept at picking up and noticing the subtleties from Japan to Europe, etc.'
>
> Chris, Executive

Gauging the level of complexity related to the size of the company is a continuous process necessary to understand how to align your team, your business unit, etc., to the larger whole. Once you are able to build a network that enables you to support your team and work-related goals, the decision-making process becomes easier. The social relationships that permit a working business relationship, however, are often open to 'cultural' misunderstanding.

> 'If you come from a European country you are used to this but if you come from a different country, it can be difficult to understand the working environment because the social connections (relationships) are not built on what you are used to.'
>
> Rajesh, Executive

Considering some of the placemaking strategies highlighted above, it is clear that relationships with one's Manager and colleagues create connections which can be used to leverage better business results. There is a 'need for highly mobile elites of management to perform boundary-spanning roles to help build social networks and facilitate the exchange of knowledge necessary to support globalization' (Farndale et al. 2009). If you are a newcomer, it can take time to build the trust needed to make changes and give new direction to a team. The ability to connect is of paramount importance and, as a Trainer, I give workshops on how to communicate effectively in order to build better relationships. There are plenty of cultural awareness courses, as well as coaching programmes on offer, due to the multinational makeup of the companies here and it is becoming increasingly important to focus on a common mission, purpose and vision for employees to engage in.

ii. Working together

Building a corporate culture that highlights the best ways of working together more effectively allows employees from diverse backgrounds to have a basic level of engagement. Corporate culture enables organisations to tackle both the difficulty of adjusting to the external environment and the internal integration of organisation resources, human resources and policies to support adapting to the external environment (Pool 2000; , 1992). Corporate culture can be viewed as the set of values, attitudes, behaviour patterns, rituals, beliefs, norms, expectations, socialisations, and employee assumptions constituting the key identity in the organisation and helping to their employees' behaviours (Schein 1992; Pool 2000).

Focusing on values and behaviours, Novartis, for example, has created a framework of Innovation, Quality, Collaboration, Performance, Courage and Integrity to recruit, develop, assess and reward people (https://www.novartis.com/our-company/our-culture-and-values). By constructing such company organisational structures as a means to implement ways of working together, there is renewed attention to the workplace. Companies now use purpose and meaning to connect individuals to their everyday work and this focus on performance ensures a commitment to the bottom line. Global competition for Talent has also increased the need to use culture as a pull factor for prospective employees. It acts as a cohesive force that unites employees around a common purpose and strategically leverages diversity for results.

My study does not allow further digression into the topic of corporate culture as a tool for building better global business outcomes. It is to be noted, however, that the companies here in Basel pride themselves on having strong organisational cultures whose processes are constantly revised and updated to promote favourable business results. My informants often talk about how aligned they are with their company objectives or how they value the 'culture of collaboration' when it comes to best practices. During the course of my research, Novartis changed its leadership and gained a new CEO. which has led to a renewed focus on culture, and Roche has also significantly transformed its organizational setup.

In addition to Bourdieu's (1986) conceptualisation of social capital as networks and resources which are supported by power and status residing in the individual, Knowledge is also a form of capital that is readily leveraged within corporate spaces as a means of professional development. Building networks that 'work for you' is a theme that strongly reproduces the stratification between employees, manifesting barriers similar to class boundaries. The relationships between the different types of capital and how they are used and transformed across the company is strategically manoeuvred through and by the company and its executives. Competition creates the need for companies to look at ways of providing equal opportunity that promote diversity and inclusion in the recruitment process. However, these have only now started coming to the fore in HR.

In his seminal work on *The Forms of Capital*, Bourdieu (1986) introduced four types of capital: economic, symbolic, social, and cultural (embodied). Political Capital, Human Capital, Emotional Capital, to name a few, have been added to this list and my dissertation also uses the word in the title. My interest is in the accrual of Capital and the way in which it can be effectively deployed by companies and individuals to serve their interests. There is an underlying question: who benefits? 'Capital, which, in its objectified or embodied forms, takes time to accumulate and which, as a potential capacity to produce profits and to reproduce itself in identical or expanded form, contains a tendency to persist in its being, is a force inscribed in the objectivity of things so that everything is not equally possible or impossible. And the structure of the distribution of the different types and subtypes of capital at a given moment in time represents the immanent structure of the social world, i.e., the set of constraints, inscribed in the very reality of that world, which govern its functioning in a durable way, determining the chances of success for practices' (Bourdieu 1986).

iii. On the Personal Front

'A good day is one without tears.'

Ann, Spouse

The stay-at-home spouse is often caught with a minimum degree of support and a lot of emotional work. What became clear to me through my data analysis was that the level of frustration and lack of support were in direct relation to an individual's flexible attitude and the ability to allow for uncertainty. Success at home is measured differently and, as one of my interviewees said, 'a good day is one without tears'. She made this strong statement when she related taking a trip to the local supermarket to buy groceries and feeling overwhelmed by her inability to find someone to help her because she could not speak any German. She could not find what she needed and then ended up back at her house in tears.

Companies here offer acculturation programmes for accompanying spouses and German language lessons. In Chapter 4, I cover the topic of German language lessons in more detail, but here it is important to note that most language lessons on offer by local providers are not for the spoken local dialect of Basel Deutsch; rather, they teach what is commonly known as High German. Spouses are offered assistance if they choose to work and yet feelings of despair can run deep. As a Coach, I have professional experience of helping the stay-at-home spouses 'pick up the pieces' of what they have left behind in terms of family support, identity, social ties, in many cases jobs or businesses. If one adds to this an overall sense of unfamiliarity with the new surroundings, it is easy to see how overwhelming this change can be. The notion of self is disrupted and needs to be created once again as they attend to the immediate needs of supporting children going to school, spouses who travel for work, and the daily experiences of family life. It is the spouse who often has to manage everything on their own in a new environment.

In Basel, the International School provides a much valued and integral point of community support for newcomers and old timers alike. The transition process for new families includes a 'host family' that is chosen from the existing parent body to provide support through the first few months or for as long as needed. Very often this turns into genuine friendship, although one of my informants did mention that she found it very strange how people of the same nationality were matched together. *'What was the point of going overseas if you only met the same kind of people?'* This ready-made social system allows for a certain degree of comfort in what is often a difficult time. The school Welcome Committee offers an array of events, such as information mornings, about where to shop and how to claim tax back for museum outings and hikes. The ties created through the school are very strong and allow for a sense of belonging in an otherwise foreign situation.

This readiness to find ways of connecting to the environment as experienced by the individual is further unpacked and analysed using *Sensorialscapes*. Using the senses as a conduit for emotions to connect to a space facilitates plugging into networks, communities, places and spaces.

iv. Affective Analysis

Whilst talking to my informants, I was often reminded of the 'emotional labour' involved in every part of the mobility trajectory, from the many considerations that went into the decision-making process, to the actual physical move and then the settling-in and orientation in a new environment. Emotions often ran high or low, and were often aplenty. It became impossible for me to ignore the feelings that accompanied each step of the process and how they affected the lived experience of individuals in a particular moment. The excitement of an overseas adventure, the sadness of goodbyes to family and friends, the frustration of packing, the trepidation of arriving and being on the other side ... each moment was described with different emotions, all playing a role in how the situation was recalled.

Affect Theory can be used to frame and articulate subjective and intersubjective states. It points to the social character of emotions. As Durkheim (1895) noted in his work *The Rules of Sociological Method*, social facts precede intention and therefore meaning. 'Social facts are defined by Durkheim as ways of acting and thinking, widely diffused in society, existing outside individual consciousness and exerting constraint upon them' (https://www.jstor.org/stable/40454241). In other words, opinions and beliefs are formed as a result of subliminal impulses and this belies how people describe situations. Anecdotes often begin with *'I did ...... because I felt ....'* Motivation appears not as a story (goal, pep talk, rallying cry) but as the forceful impulse to take action ('Cultural Anthropology: Affect an Introduction' http://orcid.org/0000-00030-2866-6587). Although it is visceral in nature, its expression, understanding, embodiment are cultural. My understanding of this reflects Bourdieu's concept of *habitus* in *The*

Logic of Practice (1990), which he describes as the outward, bodily expression of culture, 'of learned habits, bodily skills, styles, tastes, and other non-discursive knowledges that might be said to "go without saying" for a specific group' (Bourdieu 1990: 66-67). In this way, according to Brian Massumi (2015), 'the intrinsic nature of the energy that is a force within ... [is] expressed as an outward action which becomes intertwined in the moment, and upon recollection cannot be separated.' Massumi (2015: vii) calls Affect not a field of study but a 'dimension of life'. The subjectivity of this approach goes against the methodological importance most often given to objectivity and distance with regard to the positionality of ethnographers.

In 'The Potentiality of Ethnography and the Limits of Affect Theory' (Current Anthropology 54, no. S7 [October 2013]: S149-S158. https://doi.org/10.1086/670388), Emily Martin looks at the potentiality of Affect that lies deep in the human brain below the level of conscious intentionality: 'finding information in its ordinary and everyday setting' that does not rely on the tenets of rationality as the sole driver of meaning, action and belief. Sara Ahmad (2004) notes Affect's role as an intensity that variously energises, contradicts, deconstructs and overwhelms the narratives according to which we live.

The other aspect of the emotions that I would like to explore is the emotional dimension of subject and object mobility vis-à-vis cultural production and emotional interaction. This aspect of 'mobile emotions' as encapsulated in technological devices such as mobile phones, iPads, laptops, etc., allows individuals to carry and access emotions in the form of memories. The devices are ascribed with meaning beyond their object status and gain value through the emotional efficacy of images, videos, social media, etc., that they provide. The ability to access all this in transit allows individuals to be connected at a level previously only possible in person. One can argue about the depth or intimacy of such feelings but the fact remains that certain emotions are evoked and that has the effect of the indelible impression of a connection made (Svašek 2012).

v. Containing Perspectives

'What is the formula for success at your job? As a spouse? A parent? ......What is the most important dynamic of your makeup? Your Intelligence Quotient (IQ) or your Emotional Quotient (EQ)? ... Your IQ is fixed but your Emotional Intelligence (EI) which can be nurtured and developed is the real key to personal and professional growth' (S. J. Stein & H. E. Book 2000: page reference?). Whilst it can be difficult to fully capture and articulate emotions, there a lot of work has been done using EI as a tool for personal and leadership development. Social relations and interactions depend on one's ability to successfully deal with external demands and pressures. By negotiating spaces with more self-awareness, for example, connections between emotional factors and daily interactions can be optimised to achieve more positive outcomes.

This topic became relevant to my study when I was trying to better understand how certain individuals are more able to transition into a new place. As mentioned in Chapter 1, I did not look for certain groups to carry out my fieldwork. Nationality, gender, age, ethnicity, etc., were not important signifiers. Attempting to 'open' the field as much as possible, I followed the conversations and data to individual experiences. And yet, each person had a different perspective of what their journey looked like, what stood out for them, what barriers they faced. It ultimately came down to the individual vis-à-vis the emotional 'reading' of what they were going through. Since I was talking to Leaders, the language often referred to 'traits' that would ensure successful business relationships and outcomes: the Emotional Capital needed for Leadership. At the same time, the different types of Capital also allow for the successful transition of spouses to a new location; or, rather, understanding how to leverage networks in their respective spaces by using and building the necessary Capital.

At an individual level, managing emotions becomes one of the most important skills in mobility: understanding how to deal with conflicting feelings of 'being here and not there' at any given moment, crossing boundaries within oneself to accommodate the reality of the 'here and now'. The informants that were able to negotiate the inner workings of their emotions and focus on the positives through ambiguity seemed to thrive more. I therefore contend that developing resilience through understanding emotional intelligence is a key factor for success both at work and at home.

vi. Conclusion

Emotions play a vital role in our everyday lives, something that came up in my data from many different perspectives. Feelings matter and are an integral part of human consciousness and behaviour; we are feeling creatures as well as thinking creatures. Anthropologists are challenged to articulate and conceptualise theoretically what is felt and sensed. Affect Theory can be used as a description and explanation of how individuals respond to what is sensed. The task is to conceptualise the flows of mobile individuals' emotions as they Plug In and Plug Out of new spaces, sometimes using technology to assist with the maintenance of relationships, sometimes using material objects, perhaps eventually noticing that sights and smells also evoke emotions that create or rupture the feeling of belonging. I employ the concept of *Sensorialscapes* to bring together all the different sensorial elements of connecting to a space and to assess how that allows for the negotiation of familiarity in a new environment.

Treating the emotions as a tool of cultural analysis supports the idea of their being cultural expressions, socialised behaviours, 'vessels' that contain perspectives through which agency is produced. Critically, there is an ambiguity and circularity in the approach, which appears as the social manifestation of oneself within a group or space that gives meaning to whatever practice is being engaged in.

Chapter 3 : Families on the Move

Basel has a long historical connection with the Pharmaceutical Industry, promoting innovation in the research and development of drugs. Novartis, Roche & Bayer are a few of the big names that have established their corporate offices here and many other companies either form part of or support the local pharmaceutical landscape and connect it to the global network of drug suppliers.

In this chapter, I seek to understand the complex web of mobility that sees a rotation of people pass through Basel and how that impacts the company, the individual, the family and the local society. What norms are adhered to on these multiple levels by the individuals who live the experience? What factors contribute to what is deemed 'successful' and are they the same for the company, the employee, the spouse, the neighbour? Alternatively, what makes a transition difficult and what can we learn to make settling in smoother? As one HR Executive asked in conversation with me, 'is it possible to create a scale whereby we can determine whether a certain executive can make the move successfully in order to minimise cost and other negative impacts of it not working out?' Such a scale would indeed be highly desirable but when dealing with so many variables, it might be hard to construct.

> 'Well ... Carmen's job ... I mean to work with the CEO and you know do a project, specifically for him ... I mean the president ... I mean how can you say no to that ... I mean she is the hardest worker I know and she started as an Associate Director and worked her way up and then to have this role ... you know, to be in the spotlight ... really, you know, have a lot of facetime with him ... I mean to further her career obviously, and then, second, if not on the same level were the kids ... I thought "my god", I mean we lived in a beautiful area in New Jersey and it was very ... posh and the kids were very unfazed about what is going on in the world and I thought, you know, I ... to give them this opportunity to kind of get outside of this ... this easy box for them ... I thought it would be really nice ... so ...'
>
> Chloe, Spouse

The motivation for taking on an International Assignment varies from family to family. However, as the quotation above illustrates, opportunities for career growth along with the idea of expanding personal horizons are key factors. The shift to a higher skill level and expertise can lead to the often problematic decision regarding who in the couple will be the primary breadwinner, who will take care of the parental duties and, if both work, how will childcare be arranged? The sometimes ambiguous, ever-changing needs of a growing family can lead to a lot of unexpected situations and create tensions that grow bigger over time.

One of my dual career informants told me quite casually that she was so fed up with the expensive childcare costs, the lack of support and understanding of her situation from the company that they both worked for, that she was considering divorcing her husband because she was so miserable. She wondered why they would send someone to Basel from the US with 4 children and a working wife, and place them in a small apartment? It wasn't that they had a 'choice' to take the job or not, but more the understanding that this was the next step that had to be taken by her husband for his career progression.

This idea of mobility as a building block for career growth and opportunities was explained to me by an HR Manager when he shared the conception of Talent Management. The act of relocating as an individual/family requires a level of flexibility and adaptability which is necessary as a leader. Living and working in different countries creates unforeseeable challenges which in turn can add to a leader's perspective. Personal growth occurs in tandem with professional growth, which is why it is seen as a bonus. Skills are honed and added to by experiencing, establishing, understanding and observing different environments. This evolution of individual and professional strategies can be used to transfer skills across the company through best practices picked up in multiple areas/geographies. Experience gained in one location is used to groom for jobs in other locations, and this is how talent is nurtured and utilised (paraphrased from interview, 2016).

Going back to couples in which both partners work, the career trajectory of one might not match that of the other and so the choice can often be a difficult one, one spouse having to take a break. Add to that local employment regulations, language requirements, official recognition of skills and visa permits and the problem can become very tricky very quickly. The difficulty of navigating these many challenges while ensuring some semblance of normality is what the mobile family encounters and often struggles with. The link between the professional life cycle and the personal life cycle is unique to each family; however, some of the common critical decision-making points are children at university or the care of elderly parents. These two personal factors often influence career decisions with families choosing to stay grounded in one location for an extended period of time.

For companies, Talent Management is used to better understand the skills, expertise and quality of their employees in order to have the right people in the right roles. This means they need to be able to identify and measure in order to match individual and role. Put that on a global map and the variables increase tenfold. The most common approach has relied on individual relationships: Managers nominate and promote direct reports for new roles by assessing the person against the job profile. Without going into too much depth on recruitment policies, a requirement gap can create the demand for one spouse and not the other, thus forcing a decision which many are faced with: take the job or not? The emotional cost and burden often falls on the family.

i. Mobility Snapshots

Here, I will introduce my interviewees and slowly start weaving together their stories in order to highlight their mobile trajectory along with some of their motivators as well as the challenges they faced. The synthesis of all the various factors will be explored in subsequent chapters.

> Chris & Anne, American, mid-50s came to Basel on a 3-year contract and left behind their two college-aged sons in the US. They decided to bring no furniture with them and moved into a flat on the Rhine. This is their first move abroad.

The above passage is a digest from the separate interviews that I conducted with Chris and Anne and gives a very brief account of their story. I met Chris in a spacious meeting room at his workplace and he was keen for me to appreciate the beautiful surroundings and ambient atmosphere. He started off by stating that he had been with the company for a number of years and his decision to move to Basel became easier after his second son started college in the US. They didn't have to worry about schooling here, meaning that housing, the language and local Swiss culture were the main concerns. Neither of them had ever lived abroad, so it was a big move, especially for his wife, a stay-at-home mother.

> 'My experience of moving, especially to Europe, was that you should not try to export your American lifestyle. I don't think you will be successful if you come in thinking I need 2 or 3 cars, a big 2000-3000-square-foot home ... I just think you need to adapt to a more European lifestyle.'

Chris went on to relay how they decided not to bring any of their furniture with them and moved into a flat on the Rhine so that they could be in the city and walk or use public transport. The company provided a relocation agent who helped them with all the paperwork and gave them plenty of cultural insights. Chris was ready to start work from day one and felt that the physical settling-in process was smooth. He acknowledged that 'the hardest thing about coming to Basel is the language, a lot of people speak English but the receptivity improves and it helps a whole lot when you at least try to know the language.' Chris didn't have enough time to learn German and had no particular need either since he used English at work.

> 'I think the biggest thing I have learned is to adjust my expectations. It's very frustrating, between my husband and I, he goes to Novartis-land everyday where they speak English and I think about how going to the city everyday is difficult for me. Once I started German classes I had a few things I could use but before people would just walk away or say "no one can speak [English]" ... I couldn't believe it. Maybe they get tired of it here because they have a lot of cultures here ...'

> Anne, Spouse

Creating social networks for both Chris and Anne was important and the ease with which work facilitated the process was invaluable. For Anne, the spouse, however, having to build social relations through language classes was very challenging. She had to wait the whole day till her class time and then had to depend on connecting with whoever happened to be in her class.

> Patrick & Mary, Irish, late 40's here on their second stint in Basel with three teenage children, all at the International School. They moved from Ireland to Basel 10 years ago, then moved to the UK and are back in Basel again. Both work for the same company now.

I met Patrick at work on a beautiful, sunny day with sunlight streaming into the private meeting room. He was very curious about my research topic and what the findings would be, particularly since mobility is a big driver of Talent Management at multinational companies. This was his second stint at company headquarters in Basel. He shared how he had a German teacher come in three times a week and managed to learn the language in order to 'feel more comfortable' in the local environment. It was hard after a long day of work, but definitely worth it.

> 'I speak German, not Swiss German, but I fully understand it and am very well connected with my neighbours. We've been invited up to their chalets in Switzerland which is pretty unusual. We just made an effort from the start, had an Apero when we moved in, always stopped and chatted, gave presents at Christmas, just being humanistic. I feel the locals view expats that just come in and use their town for a while, don't respect them or their culture, so you'll have to break down the barriers with them and make an effort.'
>
> Patrick, Employee

It is clear that Patrick needed to find a way to form deeper relationships with his neighbours in order to connect and he used language as a tool to create his local network. The challenge of conversing in another language was something he relished: '*I started speaking as soon as I had a few sentences of German.*' He made a clear choice and an effort to show that he was integrating, and he reaped the benefits. He acknowledged that '*it is a personal journey and everyone goes through something different*'.

Mary and I met at her office on the top floor of a building overlooking the Rhine. She talked about juggling her career with young children in Ireland before they made their first move abroad. Her parents were nearby and helped with the children, but it was difficult, and Patrick worked long hours. Eventually she gave up her work in order to support the several family moves abroad.

> 'Everybody in the family moves differently and they all have different needs and different anxieties ... and certainly the man that moves very often just switches offices but somebody needs to be the stable force in the family. When you have two partners working full time, particularly expats, then somebody needs to keep the fire burning. So I got a 60% contract and have slowly adjusted as the kids have become older.'

Mary talked about the transition phase for some of the other families she met at school, particularly 'trailing spouses', who were not working. *'I met people who were completely upset that they had left their career and they were bitter, they were never going to settle here and were always resentful of the situation. By and large though, people embraced it as something different and took the time to smell the roses ... because the transition falls a lot on the trailing spouse and family to find solutions and when you are trying that in a different language, it can be challenging.'*

Carlos, Spanish, mid-30s, single. Moved to Basel 6 months before I interviewed him. This is his first move abroad.

It was a long drive for me to a site office just outside Basel to meet Carlos. He used to commute to Basel three days a week from Barcelona for several years because his ex-partner was working and did not want to leave her job. Commuting for 2 two years was hard, but they didn't have children and in the beginning it was a good compromise. Soon he became tired of the early morning flights to work or late-night departures to Barcelona and decided to move to Basel, but his partner did not join him, so they broke up.

> 'Like all Spanish guys, we contact other Spanish colleagues and are spontaneous because there are other people like you that are expat and it's easy. I mean, you know it is a different culture than mine and normally you are used to a few things, the food, the way people do things here is very strict ... the issue is language, so you need to learn German and I am trying to now but I didn't before, so I am more in the expat community and don't really have any Swiss friends, so language is a barrier. Also, I would like to

have paella and tapas, but you need to understand that if you are moving to another place you need to adapt.'

As a single person in Basel, Carlos first used his Spanish network at work to create social relationships which he later expanded to include the broader English-speaking community. Aware of cultural differences, he noted the need to learn German '*as respect and to have basic communication because I would expect the same from people who come to my country.*'

Stefanie & Thomas, German, late 40s, 2 teenage children at the Swiss International School. Been in Basel for 2 years after several international assignments, including to France and Singapore, from their base in Germany. Thomas has his own business and was sometimes working only 50% when the children were younger.

Stefanie's office was located in a newly refurbished building with lots of open space and green plants. She led me to a big conference room with all the latest teleconferencing technology for our interview. She told me that '*Basel was an easy place for her family to settle into because, as German speakers, language was no barrier. It is a very safe city and you can send your kids with the tram to school, so organising your daily life is very, very easy.*'

> 'I always feel really privileged because I always had the feeling in the first year of assignment that I am on paid vacation in a different country! For me, routine and always doing the same thing is very difficult, I am bored very quickly, so this lifestyle gives me the opportunity to learn new things. To be stretched by the assignment in my new role and to manage the family in a new environment is something very positive and I am grateful that I have the opportunity to do so, to be honest.'

When I asked Stefanie about drawbacks, she cited familial relationships, particularly feeling guilty about not being able to fully support her sister and parents. She also mentioned how difficult it is to find new friends in this life and it is the old friends that stick it out over the years. Technology, such as WhatsApp and FaceTime, has helped but it is not the same.

Rajesh & Jaya, Indian, mid-40s, 1 son. Moved to Basel from Thailand 10 months before I spoke to them and accepted another international assignment to Turkey, which they didn't know about when we spoke. This is their 7th year abroad.

Rajesh was the first person that I interviewed for this research project. He met me in his busy, open plan office and took me into a small meeting room to the side for our discussion. I remember thinking afterwards that his busy office environment reflected his open personality.

> 'Basel slowly grew on us. It wasn't a city that we fell in love with on the day we arrived here, but we asked for it [the move] because it is where the global headquarters are. We lived in exotic places like Thailand, Philippines, Vietnam, Malaysia and when the opportunity came for us to come to Basel, we said why not? In Asia, we had a huge support system with a driver, maid, big house, etc., and in Basel it was extremely difficult initially. We saw thirty houses, liked three and were rejected by all. Here, you don't choose the house, the house chooses you! Driving was a challenge but we made it our mission, so it was a slow and painful settling-in process.'

Rajesh described a key moment a few weeks before we met when he had visitors and was showing them around Basel, taking them on walks and appreciating nature together. His son had one more year to finish high school and he realised that this was the right place for his family. Jaya and I met at a coffee shop in Reinach for our interview. She was also very friendly and frank about her transition to Basel.

> 'Umm, first impressions ... well, everything is compartmentalised, sometimes very rigid, a bit overwhelming, you don't really know about the garbage bag sticker or recycling but it eventually becomes easier. At first you don't know how things function here and it's pretty black and white whereas in Asia, I could say it is grey!'

Jaya talked about learning German and how she made sure to pick up some local phrases every time she moved. She mentioned how she was already thinking about her next move because it would be without her son and the network that school provides since he would be going to university.

Lucy & Axel, British-American, mid-40s, two primary school children. Lucy was brought up 'on the move', as she says, and this is her young family's second time in Switzerland. Her American husband, a stay-at-home father, had not moved prior to their first stint abroad 6 years earlier.

Lucy and I met in her nondescript office for our conversation. As someone in HR, she was keen to share her impressions of using a moving company and having the right processes in place for mobile Corporate Executives and their families. As a working mother she uses technology to stay in touch with her young children. She, along with all of my informants, spent a lot of time communicating and maintaining long distance relationships with family and friends.

> 'I work a lot of hours and I travel a lot so I used an iPad from when they were very little to [video] call them from work so that they would not associate such calls from only when I travelled. So that's something that we do, I parent via the iPad quite a bit and discipline them when my husband is going mad, or read them bedtime stories, sing them a song to calm them down. I always want them to know that if they want me they can find me.'

Axel and I met at a coffee shop near school. He was clear about making the choice to quit his job as a personal trainer when they decided to have children because someone needed to be there for the family. He admitted to finding it hard to stay at home at first, particularly as a father but over here it was different.

> 'In the US there weren't that many fathers on the playground but over here, the Hausman group [the stay-at-home fathers' group] is quite big and diverse. There are lots of activities such as cycling, skiing, running and many get-togethers during the school day. It is quite an active bunch! I was quite surprised to see that it is much more accepted in Basel [Europe].'

Connecting with people in the same situation always helps to anchor yourself. The solidarity of a shared purpose in a new place creates bonds that help alleviate stressful situations.

Helle, German, single, early 50s. Located in Basel now after living in the US for a decade. Went there on an assignment and then moved to Basel initially for a short period and then decided to stay.

When I met Helle at her beautiful home in the Basel-Land area, she was full of energy and happy to share her story. As a German who had decided to make Basel home, it was important for her to try and bridge the gap between the local and expat communities. She volunteered for the school parent group that held the annual International Festival and her role was to act as a liaison with the local Geminde. She would deal with the bulk recycling, rubbish disposal, signage, translation, etc.

> 'For the International Festival we had to order and rent stalls, but the parents the year before I joined did not pay attention to the correct way of dismantling everything. When I asked, the complaint was that they did not listen and criss-crossed all the poles and created a lot of extra work. I was told that they [the ISB families] are very arrogant and don't care about the local community. The traffic is horrible with huge cars blocking the way. Also, you can't just hang up a banner and expect the Swiss people to show up. They need to be invited and feel welcome. Send an email to local schools or find a way to make a connection .You first have to do little steps.'

Robert & Shauna, American, late 40s, two teenagers at the International School. Five years into their first assignment abroad. Moving back to another city in the US.

I interviewed Robert at his office, which was an oasis of calm with lots of sunlight and plants. His secretary showed me in and informed me that he was on his way from another meeting.

> 'My family and I asked for this move to Basel because we thought it would be a good career opportunity for me and also good timing for the family. So, on a personal level, you have to have the family piece in place, otherwise the company piece won't work. The family has to be ready for it. Knowing that your family is not happy, you cannot be successful at work. You need to have that support from your spouse and children, particularly if you are in a new country.'

He noted that the move made sense with his school-aged children and now that his wife was not working. The plan was to move back to the US for high school so that the children could build the social networks that would see them into college.

Carmen & Chloe, American, mid-40s, first assignment abroad. Two middle school children at the International School.

Carmen was very welcoming when she ushered me into her new office. It was airy and light with lots of pictures on the sideboard. We spent some time discussing the different ways of doing business and how working together effectively is something that everyone needs to work on in order to keep pushing for better results.

> 'Coming from the US, everybody told me about Sundays and how quiet they are in Basel. Everything is closed and it is sold as "good family time" and we laugh because you can get a little sick of each other! But really, people say it either brings you closer together as a family or puts extra stress. We changed our lifestyle here and got the kids to be much more active outside.'

Chloe and I met at a coffee shop in town. She was happy to be a stay-at-home mum and enjoyed her supportive role.

> 'We did a lot of the holiday celebrations at our house back in the US. This past Christmas was our first one here and it was awful. Like December 15, school was done so everybody just left! It was so weird. Gone till January! And then the food is so different, the ingredients I am used to are hard to find and I love cooking. It's better now that I go to Carrefour or Hieber but I still don't know what everything is! It's all in French or German and how much can you Google Translate? I mean it's crazy just doing something simple like grocery shopping!'

ii. Conclusion

The emotional toll and uncertainty of displacement is something that came up in nearly every interview. Making sense of a new environment places a huge amount of stress on the individual or on every member of the family unit in different ways. Responsibility for the children and the school environment, as well as the 'loneliness' of having to 'keep it all together' for the sake of the family, often falls on the accompanying spouse. Small tasks such as finding the ingredients for favourite recipes can lead to a gamut of emotions and become markers of adjustment success or failure.

I heard countless stories regarding the German language, the reasons for learning it or not and the kind of daily interactions people had with the local community. The difficulties of negotiating the language barrier required the development of coping strategies, which would allow getting through everyday tasks with the minimum amount of 'tears', 'stress' and 'frustration'. The significance of Language as a means of belonging and feeling settled was not lost on my interviewees. Conflicting emotions and anxieties experienced during relocation are often underestimated by companies and families alike.

'International assignments constitute a proven method for developing global managers. Most senior managers have extensive international experience. The managers' various international experiences help in developing a global understanding of the organization. Moreover, international transfers develop the individual's commitment toward the organization, his or her feeling of belonging and loyalty. Organizations that use expatriation to improve their managers' competencies, either formally or not, associate expatriation with promotions' (Waxin 2007: page reference). When it is clear that company and career requirements require a move due to the very nature of global management practices, often there is very little choice.

The Mobility Snapshots above highlight some of the conflicting choices families are driven to make in narratives that present the experiences of the informants as they grapple with the personal and professional relationship between mobility and success.

Chapter 4 : Intellectual Capital as Currency

Intellectual Capital as a skill can be translated in to career capital by individuals. It is commodified by companies and is used by individuals to negotiate career opportunities. International Assignments are sought-after experiences that can accelerate career trajectories. Many of the Corporate Executives I spoke with openly discussed their professional growth in terms of mobility. Experience abroad is indicative of the ability to adapt to new environments and develop cross-cultural skills. Multinational companies deploy executives to cross-pollinate ideas and practices between different geographical locations. Different management styles and skills are used to enhance Leadership skills with the tacit understanding that having 'proved yourself' in a different environment is a necessary and important accrual of Intellectual Capital. It is therefore unsurprising that mobility is used as a strategy for career advancement by both the employee and employer.

> 'Well ... Carrmen''s job ... I mean to work with the CEO and you know do a project, specifically for him...I mean the president...I mean how can you say no to that ... I mean she is the hardest worker I know and she started as an Associate Director here in Novartis and worked her way up and then to have this role...you know, to be in the spotlight ... really, you know, have a lot of facetime with him ... I mean to further her career obviously and then second, if not on the same level were the kids ... I thought "my god", I mean we lived in a beautiful area in New Jersey and it was very ... posh and the kids were very unfazed about what is going on in the world and I thought, you know, I ... to give them this opportunity to kind of get outside of this ... this easy box for them ... I thought it would be really nice ... so ...'
>
> Chloe

Corporate Executive Mobility is often seen as a way to enhance leadership skills, transfer knowledge and skills, and increase diversity in the workplace (S. Baert, CHRO Novartis). It is seen as a necessary qualification and resource for career development. The 'openness to new experiences' (Hannerz 1996), which informs the initial motivation to move, brings into play the personal and the professional, highlighting the lure of an international assignment. 'Mobility changes you as a Leader, it redefines your life' (S. Baert).

In addition to focusing on organisational business objectivities, companies looking for greater diversity in their workforce bring new perspectives through work placements in different geographies. Their corporate mobility policies create both dependency and vulnerability. There is economic uncertainty, because a smaller proportion of overseas jobs are for life, and the accompanying spouse's earning potential often diminishes with time, making it more important for the corporate employee to be successful. The accompanying spouse's multiple roles, which include managing the household, taking care of the children, and providing emotional support to their spouse as the latter adjusts to an organisation in a new setting, often comes at a cost.

Whenever I talked about my research group with people not in my field, in the larger Basel community, they would use terms like 'elite' and 'privileged expatriates'. It is often assumed that they have an 'easy life'. In her book *The Trailing Spouse Reimagined* (2018), co-authored with Adriana Quarck and Francesca Incocciati, Rylla Resler recounts 'Stories of People Transported by Love'. She herself moved to Basel over a decade ago because of her husband's work and interviewed dozens of men and women who did the same. The book explores 'the challenges and true joys of life abroad'. In my conversations with her, she talked about how she wanted to 'inspire' people with 'stories of uprooted lives'. In the foreword of the book, Dr Tanja Popovic, Head of the Welcome Center at the University of Basel, writes: 'These men and women who "trail along" soon get to know the joys and challenges of their move: the frustrations of integrating into a new culture; periods of euphoria and great curiosity; the highs and lows of intense self-reflection; the openness of a Global life and the narrowness of the closed communities of expats; rejection and crisis; and stress in their relationship, which often leads to a new closeness with their partners. This emotional rollercoaster is tiring, but because of it, many people develop completely new — and often unexpected — ways of life.'

'Spend time talking to them [the employee] about their children and their partner. That's the tough element. The job is fine, you are appreciated for the skill you are bringing, there is a structure associated with it, you can assess whether you want the job at the interview, you are somewhat energised. But when you are at work, you have children who are trying to figure out what this is all about, who are put in a situation not because of their choice. You have a partner who is dealing with all of that and going through emotions, also made some sacrifices, so I would be asking questions about their children and partner. If they have not thought about this then it would indicate to me that they need to think about it more.'

Patrick, Executive

In this quotation, Patrick probed the motivations of prospective employees during the interview process. We had a wide-ranging discussion about how important it is for both spouses to be aware of the impact of their decision at a deeper level. He went on to note that if an employee's family is not happy at home, it affects his work. He said that he always shares his own experiences of moving with a family and tries to emphasise that 'the impact on the partner is huge and significant and they carry a lot on their shoulder'. He felt that the very often the candidate had not fully thought out the implications of a move. He recounted the case of one of his team members, who came to him 6 months after moving to say that he was separating from his wife and wished that he had given the matter more thought. The breakdown of family units is something that I have personally witnessed over the years.

If Intellectual Capital is used as currency, it has different meanings for the different stakeholders. Recognising the complexity of the situation requires a great deal of self-reflection on the part of families. Companies have now taken a more nuanced approach to managing their mobile talent pool. I have added the family dynamic to the discussion on Intellectual Capital because, whilst it is the employee who technically holds the Capital, the spouse and family are critical to the success of the assignment as 'invisible participants' in the process.

'The psychological perspective of the adjustment process emphasises the emotions felt at the time, such as: anxiety, frustration, homesickness, satisfaction, as well as the problem of stress frequently accompanying international assignments (Torbion 1982; Brown 2008: 1018-1034). A spouse interacts with the local society more frequently, must often give up his/her career and does not have such opportunities to sustain relationships or receive support in the professional sphere as the expatriate who cooperates with the parent firm − usually in a more familiar environment, resembling home organisation in terms of corporate values and job characteristics. The spouse is more vulnerable to culture shock, as it is the expatriate who often works in the international teams where people widely speak English, whereas the spouse has more frequently to do with people who don't belong to this cosmopolitan elite' (Andreason 2008).

It is this understanding that drives companies to offer support, such as relocation services, language lessons and cultural training, to their senior executives and their families. It forms some of the necessary Capital for the move.

i. Language as Currency

The relevance of locality for the mobile group in this study is revealed by the everyday practices of life in Basel. The experience of the host country may be perceived through an outsider lens, particularly when language is a barrier.

> 'It's very frustrating ... between my husband and I ... which I'll say, he goes to Novartis-Land every day ... beautiful ... I mean it's like going to ... I mean it's so beautiful there ... they all speak English ... if he said ... if he needs to, like, "hey, I need to know where to go to get someone who would help him", you know ... so that ... would be the difference ... and I think his perspective of ... you know, he may walk to the work and back ... he may ... you know ... but he doesn't notice, the difference ... um ... and I think for me going into the city everyday it's very difficult ... and ... some ... some people would help me ... some people would not ... once I started taking German classes then the more I could choose ... I used to ... I always try to use something ... but ... but without having any of it, was really impossible ... I mean I would have people walk off, say "no one can speak ... no one can ..." I mean literally, no one can help you or just ... just walk off and not even say anything ... you just kind of be ...'

Anne

Communication is key to forming relationships with others and also to understanding the environment. Linguistic Anthropology delves deeply into the subject of language and culture, looking at meanings and symbols as described by the speakers of a particular language, but this area does not lie within my research remit. The evidence I have is more anecdotal, personal and evocative of experiences, interactions, and self-reflections on how to navigate the local Basel landscape.

> 'I think, if you're here on your own that can contribute to unhappiness ... if you're not out there included in some sort of network ... if you're so hung up on the foods that you had at home, the way the things were done at home ... some Americans in particular, because I think Europeans transition better to Switzerland than Americans ... depending on the Americans ... but if you're used to even ... you know, even in the States in the last [?] huge volume of packaging and etc., etc. ... and the big cars and the big supermarkets and the big trolley ... suddenly all that's gone ... and you've a small Migros or a small Coop and ... that's ... that's not everybody's ... uh ... comfort zone and then if you need certain ingredients and you can't find them here, 'cause you're going to the store and everything is written in German ... I mean, a very intelligent friend of mine said she cried in Coop once, 'cause she was looking for something to clean her sink and didn't know where to start [laugh] ... and they are the small things that break you ... now, if you can turn around and laugh at yourself after that .. .that's fine.I would just accept it ... that it's part of the move ... but if it's you first move .... it's a lot more dramatic.'
>
> Mary

After negotiating a different language and culture, there seems to be a gain in understanding the process, particularly after multiple moves. So does it become easier and, if it does, what helps to make it easier? The motivations for and perceived advantages of mobility do not make the act and experience any easier, especially for the accompanying spouse. What emerged from my data to this point was the complexity relocating added to family life and how the 'emotional labour' (Yeoh et al. 2005) falls on the homemaker, regardless of gender. Is learning the language also part of the Capital accrual process?

My informants spoke of Cosmopolitanism (Beck 2000) as 'accepting other cultures', being 'open-minded'. It acts as a privileged notion to reflect 'global-mindedness' and the ability to switch between cultural codes comfortably. Yet I found that many of these people still cluster around language and nationality. The groups in the playground at the International School show this demarcation pretty clearly. And whilst people mix and profess to have friends from different countries, their deep social networks revolve around nationality and the ease of conversing in a particular language. Does this feeling dissipate at some point, after multiple moves, or maybe through the 'disconnection of networks' over time? Or maybe even through the conscious accumulation of certain kinds of Capital?

Emotions seem to play a huge role in the process and this is where the concept of Translocal Subjectivity comes into play. The commitment to family, friends and community in particular locations, and negotiating the means to practise and maintain relationships, is key to self-identity and meaning for mobile persons (Conradson & McKay 2007). and these are reflected in some of the emotions and strategies of mobility exemplified in my data. Negotiating change in a new setting requires multiple layers of different strategies and the ability to accept that things will be different, maybe even difficult, at first requiring resilience, an open mind and patience. Although creating and maintaining social networks is key, mobility is often experienced as a lonely process.

'The biggest thing that I have learned is adjusting my expectations.'

Anne

Conclusion

The emotional condition of mobile people and the way that condition informs identity and belonging over time and space through sensorial practices was highlighted time and again in my research. The senses are seen as vessels of meaning that are culturally constructed and transmitted vertically down the generations and horizontally across geographical locations, particularly in this increasingly globalised world.

Arjun Appadurai writes about global cultural flows in his seminal work on globalisation, classifying the different ways in which the social imaginary is created through social practices that are articulated through mediascapes, ideascapes, ethnoscapes, technoscapes and financescapes (Appadurai 1996; Appadurai 2002). These flows are exchanged, expressed, negotiated and created at all levels by people who are able to engage and reproduce their own version. Whilst it is clear that there are local, national, supranational, governmental and other factors involved in this process, I do not to assess the level of agency an individual has vis-à-vis structures and institutions since this lies outside of the scope of my research. What was highlighted time and again in my interviews and extensive fieldwork is the way in which the senses participate in the creation of 'everydayness' in localised and displaced communities such as the mobile families forming my research group.

Flows are easily captured via technology, through the 'mediated mobility' of smartphones and computers, resulting in locally produced and deliberately maintained practices that are expressed in patterns of consumption, style, taste, etc., actions that signal and inform daily lives. Globalisation manifests itself locally in different forms. The contexts derived from the lived experience of my informants reflect the flows involved in the creation of a daily rhythm of work and family life. By looking at particular aspects of daily life such as food, rituals, emotions, space/place creation, material culture, etc., I examine how the senses interact with the creation of *Sensorialscapes*. I have coined this concept to capture 'connecting oneself to a space through sensorial mobility, the five senses and memory, to create an embodied experience which individuals use to negotiate belonging in a new environment.'

Chapter 5 : Mobility Flows: Emotions; Food, Rituals, Memory

In this chapter, I explore Mobility Flows vis-à-vis Scapes as outlined by Arjun Appadurai in his seminal work on Globalisation. The five Scapes of Global Cultural Flows —dEthnoscapes, Ideoscapes, Technoscapes, Financescapes and Mediascapes — theorise the interconnection and movement of people, goods, ideas, information, technology and money across national boundaries (Appadurai 1996). Appadurai's work expands the discourse regarding influencing factors and the interrelatedness of cultures across the globe. *Sensorialscapes* incorporate memory and rituals to connect across time and space, using food, objects, relationships, etc., to form meaningful bonds through performance. Today, it is clear that technology connects us even more closely and that these Scapes function in real time.

> *'It's an effort ... especially for us ... it's a 6-hour time difference ... it's hard for the kids ... you know, it's like weekends we have to make sure that we try calling friends back home ... you know, Facebook ... you know, again ... it's a little bit easier, we're always keeping in touch, but ... uh ... but with the kids, like by the time their friends come home from school at 4 o'clock it's like 10 o'clock here ... so it's .. it's hard ...'*
>
> Chloe

The issue of maintaining relationships as a result of relocation may be considered a private matter, however, the impact upon employee performance as a result of poor family adjustment to a new environment cannot be underestimated. Social networks need to be constantly reinforced and maintained in order to continue to have ties with friends and relatives that live far away. Many issues crop up as a result of the 'hard work' involved in the practice of 'keeping in close touch' and the realisation of how social relations are affected. Mobility affects the ways in which lives are lived, experienced and understood, and the ways in which identities are constituted, performed and organised across different spaces and through time (Urry 2007). I note that the emotions play a major role in the complexity of mobile family life.

Relationships nowadays rely heavily on technology for 'virtual co-presence' (Baldassar 2007), which allows for the simultaneous management of social networks locally and internationally, making it easier to stay connected with loved ones. However, as already asked earlier, is it the rule that the fewer ties you have, and the weaker that they are, the easier it is to be mobile (Nowicka, 2005)? The co-existence of deep connections in multiple locations is viewed by some as a 'blessing', and a sense of community with other mobile individuals, who have completely different life trajectories, through recognition of themselves in each other's stories (Svašek 2008), helps create bonds locally.

The ability to connect is therefore one of the nodes that operate on multiple levels in an individual's adjustment process, both internally and externally. Its importance recognised. However, the loss of a past life with its familiar patterns and the need to reproduce those patterns in a new environment are sometimes difficult to reconcile. As my findings show, language plays a major role in the ability to connect to the local community here in Basel. The confusion, frustration and helplessness experienced in everyday encounters often leads the less resilient members of the international community to just stay within their own limited network. This in turn leads to feelings of alienation, which are expressed through continued refusal to learn German or indignation that Swiss people will not speak English even though they can. It is important to note that this attitude, on both sides, serves only to further disconnect communities in the same city. Contact with family and friends abroad, therefore, seems to be the lifeline that allows a certain level of independence from the host community, and also serves as an emotional conduit for positivity and assurance during the uncertain first few months of the relocation process.

i. Affect Theory Unpacked

An understanding of the frame Affect Theory uses to examine and articulate subjective and intersubjective states allows for a deeper probing of some key aspects of human behaviour, namely what is felt and sensed. It is challenging to conceptualise theoretically both the idea that human beings interact with the environment around them through the senses and how that interaction shapes meaning and practice. Feelings matter and are an integral part of human consciousness and behaviour. The description and éxplanation of Affect allows for 'thick description' (Geertz 1973) and considers how 'Affects are communicative and do not reside within individual bodies, but exist as a relation between subjects, and between subjects and things or symbols' (Wise & Velayutham 2017: page reference).

The importance of locating an individual's practices and motivations through the relational participation in everyday activities, activities that constitute the 'familiar' daily rhythm of 'feeling settled' in a place, was highlighted to me in nearly every interview and spontaneous conversation. The idea emerged that mechanisms can be used to ground oneself in a particular space, often through translocating a familiar sensorial activity such as eating a particular food or seeing a movie in your native language. I started to explore sensorial mobility as a translator of the embodied experience, which included memory, to create a sense of 'rootedness' and 'belonging'. People engage with sensorial experiences to locate and understand themselves within a certain space and this in turn gives meaning and value based on perceptions conditioned by culture. This is the symbolic value of sensorial practices; it gives cultural meaning.

> 'It's a huge thing being able to cook what I used to cook back home, I love cooking and the kids ... it makes a big difference to them just seeing those dishes again. Like there were some of the ingredients here I couldn't figure out like buttermilk, flour, steaks are so expensive ... our first Christmas here was awful, so weird. No one was in town and I missed my family gathering in Florida. I didn't cook a proper meal so after that experience we either had family over or went somewhere ourselves.'
>
> Chloe

The emotions evoked through food created transnational connections by the performance of eating home-cooked meals together. These were a reminder of what they had before moving. Celebrations and holidays such as Thanksgiving and Christmas embody home whilst abroad thanks to clear markers of rituals that connect through materiality, emotion and social bonds. Evoking memories through traditions that require particular objects — food, decorations, presents, smells, music, etc. — is an example of how *Sensorialscapes* can be practised. 'Cultures travel as well as people' (Rojek and Urry 1997:11). In her article, 'The Object of Christmas: The Politics of Festive Materiality in the Lives of Polish Immigrants', Kathy Burrell writes: 'Emotions are now widely understood as a subjective interaction (Lutz 1986) between the inner self and the outside world, and Svašek (2009) suggests that there are three different ways this process is manifested through discourse, practice and embodied experience. Baldassar (2008) also includes a further category in her work: that of imagination and ideas' (Burrell 2014).

ii. Sensorial Mobility

Following on the prevalence of emotions that are socially and culturally (re)constructed through mobility, I found myself looking at how my informants embodied their experiences and how they used this knowledge to navigate their new environment. According to Hannerz (1996: 109) this 'decontextualised knowledge [which] can be quickly and shiftingly recontextualised in a number of settings' is the Cultural Capital that makes settling in easier. Although often analysed within the framework of materiality, my research highlighted how the commodification of emotions can benefit individuals when choosing to relocate. Those with the ability to negotiate ambiguity and deal with uncertainty often found it easier to adjust to a new environment. Leaders with this skill are earmarked for success.

The exploration of how the senses influence our ability to interact with the environment around us is not new. However, the idea that this still often overlooked aspect can influence our experience in settling down became very clear to me through my interviews. The search for ingredients to cook a favourite dish in order to celebrate Thanksgiving, for example, struck me as quite telling. On the surface, this should be quite easy since it involved no more than going to the grocery store, buying certain ingredients and then cooking the said dish. American families come together and celebrate this holiday by giving thanks and cooking a somewhat 'staple' menu of Turkey, stuffing, cranberry sauce, some vegetable sides and pumpkin pie.

'Memory is stored in substances that are shared just as substances are stored in social memory, which is sensory' (Serematakis 1994). The act of gathering together at Thanksgiving to reproduce a ritual grounded in the communal act of eating highlights the subjective meaning of food. It is much more than nourishment of the physical body. 'Food is imbued with moral and social meaning' (Douglas 1984). There is a strong relation between the emotions, memory and food preferences, particularly when it comes to significant moments such as holidays or celebrations. There is an emotional bond not only between the individual and food, but also between individuals and absent others whose memory the food evokes. Food allows one to reconnect to certain spaces and people by reliving the memory of sharing the food eaten. In certain ways, food contains the history of our mobility because it can link back to our personal story and mirror how we have changed over space and time. Particular foods become associated with certain events, people or spaces and can therefore be used to mould emotions.

Eating is an experience that is inherently synaesthetic, the stimulation of one sense evoking the experience of another sense. Simply reading a recipe can make your mouth water! The 'cultural shaping of the senses' (Korsmeyer & Sutton 2015) allows us to explore and understand the gustemological organisation of social life through food and the senses. These form some of the categories that shape our perception of the world. Both memory and sense-making are conceptualised as active, creative and transformational cultural processes. This approach helped me better understand my informants' need to source special ingredients to cook foods that are 'family favourites'.

According to Srinivas (2006), global food flows construct identity in a cosmopolitan and multicultural world. The social and symbolic contours of transnational food are enacted through consumption (Berger 1961). Food can be a marker of identity, particularly when there is a nostalgic desire to prepare food in order to keep tradition alive for the children. There are complex connections between culture, parenthood, family dynamics, food consumption and identity. This complexity is amplified by family relocation, when 'homemaking' is constructed in an unfamiliar environment. Food plays a significant part in evoking a multifaceted experience of place, connecting the here and now to what was and what will be. Perception and memory connect the body with material culture and articulate often unexplored experiences in ethnography.

iii. Emotional Capital

The emotions are socially and culturally (re)constructed, and underlie the behaviours of individuals, often determining their choices. They form the basis of human interaction with the environment and are an expression of the senses. Migration entails the full gamut of emotions such as hope, adventure, longing, nostalgia, ambition, guilt, etc., and interacts with the everyday relationships that are formed through the many interactions before and after a move. How these emotions and experiences play out and are negotiated by individuals is often overlooked by organisations. Whilst relocating is acknowledged as a sometimes 'difficult' process, the economic benefits along with the positive career prospects often outweigh the 'emotional labour' involved. The effort to reconcile the reality of life in a new environment with the sense of displacement stay-at-home spouses often feel weighed heavily on the minds of everyone I engaged with. Derailers can sometimes be small incidents that cause great upset. (Boccagni 2015; Baldassar 2007).

'I think Europeans transition better to Switzerland than Americans ... depending on the Americans ... but if you're used to even ... you know, even in the States in the last [?] huge volume of packaging and etc., etc. ... and the big cars and the big supermarkets and the big trolley ... suddenly all that's gone ... and you've a small Migros or a small Coop and ... that's ... that's not everybody's ... uh ... comfort zone and then if you need certain ingredients and you can't find them here, ''cause you're going to the store and everything is written in German ... I mean, a very intelligent friend of mine said she cried in Coop once, ''cause she was looking for something to clean her sink and didn't know where to start [laugh]...and they are the small things that break you ... now, if you can turn around and laugh at yourself after that ...that's fine.I would just accept it ... that it's part of the move ... but if it's you first move .... it"s a lot more dramatic.'

Mary

It helps to focus on the emotional lives of migrants at the individual, household and community levels, as well as to take into consideration national and transnational social fields (Levitt & Glick Schiller 2004) and scapes (Appadurai 1996) of lived experience, as this provides further tools to analyse practices and interactions over distance, time and space. Mobility in this technological day and age adds a further level of complexity to the way belonging, home and identity are negotiated. The level of ambiguity, ambivalence and emotional connection across boundaries is often underestimated. Change and transformation at the individual level inform social orientation and relationships that create a supra-national community and bonds.

Technological advancement has added to the multiple levels of 'connection' that are available and contributes to the flows of emotions across time and space. Social ties are easier to maintain through mobile phone usage, for example, and the idea of 'co-presence' explored by Baldassar (2007) attune participants to a shared present experience running from routine moments such as dinner to events such as a graduation. These moments of long distance affective interaction underpin the mobile experience of individuals, carrying emotions via text message, picture, Facetime, WhatsApp, etc. Instant connection via these tools serves to supply the emotional stability often required by migrants to anchor themselves in the comfortable feeling of belonging. Technology makes it possible to be connected enough to share and experience the everyday rhythm and routine that fosters social ties.

> 'Lack of stability, a huge amount of change, I think has the potential to really strengthen the family bond because we have to stick together and so routines are really important for our girls to have some security in that. I travel a lot and so I parent using the iPad and call them from wherever I am and read them a bedtime story as part of their routine, maybe sing them a song if they are upset, calm them down, so they are used to me not always being there but being accessible so that they can always reach me.'
>
> Lucy

The above account illustrates one of the multiple ways in which virtual co-presence can be utilised to good effect, ensuring the involvement of a parent who is away travelling on business, or perhaps simply having a long day at work, maintaining a close emotional connection through the use of technology. As a full-time working mother with a demanding career, Lucy was happy to use the tools available to 'parent from a distance' and provide the 'emotional stability' she felt her children needed. It also allowed her to feel more involved in their daily routines.

Emotions are social and cultural in that they are created and understood intersubjectively. We respond to and communicate with the environment through our emotions. Individuals align and attach to their communities through Affect (Ahmed 2004a: 119). Sensorial mobility explores the process of reproduction through embodied experience. Sensing the world is the first stage of making sense of it (Classen 1997). It provides a framework for the symbolic value of sensorial practices. Through the senses, we are able to connect on multiple levels and create the bonds required to locate ourselves in space. The meaning attached to certain objects, foods, sights, smells, along with their sensorial relationships, act as connectors across time and space. A Christmas meal in Basel evokes distinct emotional reactions among those participating in the ritual celebration. The performance not only includes a meal, but often an exchange of presents, decorations, music, smells, family/friends, thus creating bonds between the participants as well as the objects and also with the 'memory' of what a traditional Christmas celebration is (Svašek 2014).

iv. Emotions on the Move

Experiences and practices capture the meaning behind what is observed. Agency is the individual response set within larger institutional structures that can either enable or disable the construction of the social. The *Sensorialscape* of personal experiences is created by taking embodied experience and using the senses, including memory, to connect and create the ability to 'Plug In' to locate oneself in a space. Memory is the powerful 'sense' that provides the link between past and present experiences, allowing for sensorial mobility to transcend time and space. Various strategies can be used to Plug In to the local, such as food, smells, sights and sounds. Restaurants are a particularly good example of how the senses can be used to create a *Sensorialscape* that captures a particular cultural ambience through food, music and décor. The focus of my study does not allow for further analysis of this idea. However, data clearly revealed the informants' search for and creation of spaces that connected them to the familiar.

The search for particular ingredients to cook 'family favourites' was a regular topic of conversation amongst my informants. Tips and tricks on where to source special items are often posted in online forums especially before holidays such as Christmas, Thanksgiving, Easter, etc. Food is used to communicate belonging and though, again, this study does not permit further discussion of the anthropological bonds on display, the lived experience of mobile individuals highlights the fundamental character of this phenomenon.

Memory allows for the replication of activities through which a tradition is kept alive. Through remembering we actively engage in connecting past and present, anchoring ourselves and our emotions in rituals such as special foods, decorations and gatherings. For mobile populations, this need to connect with the familiar and comfortable through objects containing social and emotional qualities is well documented. Stories and experiences uphold traditions across time and space.

The role of materiality as a means to construct *Sensorialscapes* in everyday routines, as well as for special celebrations, is of the utmost importance. For example, certain foods and objects can be replicated by cooking favourite dishes and performing 'family activities' that signify occasions such as Christmas, Thanksgiving, Easter, Eid, birthdays, etc., each of these activities requiring the procurement of particular items to (re)produce familiar experiences that resonate with the participants on an emotional level, (re)creating social bonds. The significance of observing these moments and thus being able to fully participate is often what facilitates a sense of home. The presence or absence of 'emotionally charged' objects affects the meaning of the experience for the participants.

The ability of individuals who adopt the mobile lifestyle to 'Plug Out' of a space is important. They often display the fluid ability to extract themselves from a space by using their emotions to create a link between past and present. There is a certain intentionality in being able to make a seamless transition. I contend that this flexibility is one of the key characteristics of a successful mobile lifestyle.

v. Conclusion

Modelled on Appadurai's Globalisation scapes, I use *Sensorialscapes* to highlight the flow of emotions as embodied and practised by mobile individuals by connecting to a space via the senses. This ability to Plug In by linking a meaningful emotion to a sense, thus creating the familiar cultural practice, allows for the reproduction of patterns embodying home and belonging. *Sensorialscapes* are thus powerful signifiers of connection and adjustment. Although it is clear that they cannot truly replicate the 'real' experience, the performance or reminder evokes strong feelings of connection across boundaries. This transmission of cultural values through the senses allows for flows of meaning in mobile individuals.

Once *Sensorialscapes* are used intentionally, the continuous process of coming to terms with a mobile lifestyle becomes easier. The sensorial aspects of cultural practices, in particular those connected with modern-day mobilities, increase familiarity and adjustment. The senses are seen here as vessels of meaning – culturally constructed and transmitted vertically, down the generations, and horizontally, across geographically enclosed cultural entities, and linked to migration movements and the increasing information exchange of a globalized world. Therefore, the role of the senses in establishing identity through cooking and eating practices, making home and material culture, as well as through rituals and performances, demonstrates that the senses participate in the creation of everydayness in localized and displaced communities, and allows for a better understanding of practices and behaviours.

Chapter 6 : Transnational Transformations

Mobility as lived experience varies greatly from individual to individual, narrative to narrative. The focus for an employee will be different to that of the accompanying spouse and of course the Company. The aligning of interacting priorities and considerations has been much discussed, as can be seen from the discourse so far. What of the Transnational networks that are formed as a result? At every level, technological advancements enable global connections that are used to support work initiatives as well as personal matters and allow for much deeper and closer ties. How are these different aspects leveraged and understood by the actors?

In this chapter I seek to further explore some of the strategies by different stakeholders to connect both locally and transnationally, focusing in particular on the emotions and on different forms of Capital. The ability to accumulate the desired resources to negotiate different facets of the lived of experience is a matter of keen interest. 'Adjustment, which has been defined as an individual's degree of comfort, familiarity and ease with several aspects of a new cultural environment, is considered to play a central role in expatriation success' (Davoine & Claudio 2013: page reference).

i. Management Matters

'As three trends — complexity, speed to market, and global reach — converge, the need for competent managers to take on cross-border assignments grows. This is where global mobility fits in. Effective global mobility strategy and execution — or strategic global mobility — can be a key tenet of organizational effectiveness and performance management. By tying global mobility strategy to other metrics, best-in-class organizations have reported their global mobility programs have been critical to supporting new business growth, improving financial performance, bolstering employee engagement, succession planning, retaining and developing top talent, and increasing diversity' (Harvard Business Review: Strategic Global Mobility 2014).

Talent Management, Diversity & Inclusion, Learning & Development as well as Organisational Development are some of the focal areas of HR policies. Research & Development of Drugs, Data Analytics — in fact, all areas of the Pharmaceutical Industry, and indeed all multinational companies — now rely on global networks for a flow of people with new ideas that can add a competitive edge and increase profit share. 'Why use international employees? Reasons vary from one multinational organization to the other, but an analysis of the literature suggests that international employees fulfill five major roles. The first three roles are tactical in nature: fulfilling a need for a certain type of personnel that is not available in the host country, sharing and transferring information, and developing the capacities and level of implication of managers within the organization. The other two roles are strategic in nature: controlling and coordinating activities' (Waxin 2007).

> 'It was a very different type of work so it took me a year to understand what kind of impact you can have and what does success look like ... And to navigate here in the matrix environment, to build your network, it takes a while to understand and see what you need to leverage and what are the opportunities ... It's a very, very different environment at headquarters. I mean, compared to other companies, I think the company is passionate about culture and having a positive, inspiring, welcoming culture and thinking about it a lot. To speak up, have courage, more opportunities to collaborate, I think we have come a significant way but we still have some way to go.'
>
> Stefanie

Settling into the work rhythm at headquarters often involves a steep learning curve for many of the Executives that are transferred to Novartis Basel, as noted in the above quotation. The matrix of buildings that make up the primary campus is a physical manifestation of the many operational and structural silos that operate there. I cover the typography of some of the companies in Basel in Chapter 7, where I also explore the makeup of Basel as a city. Here, I use Novartis as an example to show how the company has spent time intentionally creating a culture that is exemplified through its Values and Behaviours (see Figure 3, below). Company culture is seen as a key component of success. 'A positive work environment boosts all workers, leading to an increased productivity across all aspects of your business. Furthermore, a positive culture and environment helps you retain your employees, ensuring that your most valuable assets stick around' (http://davidmilberg.net/growing-business-company-culture-key/).

The preferred attributes of company culture at Novartis are outlined in the list of Novartis Values and Behaviours, which is prominently displayed on boards at various locations across the Basel campus. I have noted these displays at every Novartis location across Europe that I have visited on professional training visits. Each Personal Effectiveness Programme (PEP) training workshop that I have delivered — whether Resolving Conflict and Disagreement, Communicate to Connect, Design Thinking Fundamentals etc. — refers to these Values and Behaviours as points of reference for the preferred professional profile and method of interaction within the company: the cultural behaviours that need to be adopted for success at work. Using training to share, discuss and disseminate certain soft skills that can be actively adopted and developed by individuals is one way of devloping the mindset that leads to sought-after Leadership Skills such as effective professional communication. This dissemination of culture, present in the ubiquitous reminders, exhibits and also, through training opportunities, helps to build a practice of shared commonalities across the multinational workforce spanning a global network of offices.

Opportunities to leverage the company culture to gain best practices are manifold. Company culture provides the basis for learning and for the development of employees through training initiatives. It also serves as a way to set business objectives and Leadership goals, and forms the basis of professional workplace interactions. Assessment tools for Emotional Intelligence, Communication Styles, Leadership Profiles, etc. are built on company culture: an endless series of methods linking the internal 'purpose' of individuals to the external 'mission' of the company. Through a combination of all of the above, the pathway to career success appears connected to personal development, an understanding of company culture, in addition to Intellectual Capital, i.e. job-related expertise.

Novartis Values & Behaviors

	What we value	Observed behaviors
Patient & Customer	**Innovation** by experimenting and delivering solutions	Experiments and encourages others to do so Takes smart risks that benefit patients and customers Delivers new solutions with speed and simplicity
	Quality by taking pride in doing ordinary things extraordinarily well	Is always looking for better ways to do things Does not compromise on quality and safety and strives for excellence Continuously works to improve own strengths and weaknesses
Team	**Collaboration** by championing high performing teams with diversity and inclusion	Champions working together in high performing teams Knows self and impact on others Welcomes diversity and inclusion of styles, ideas and perspectives
	Performance by prioritizing and making things happen with urgency	Is passionate to achieve goals, goes the extra mile Puts team results before own success, acknowledges contribution of others Prioritizes, decides and makes things happen with urgency
Self	**Courage** by speaking up, giving and receiving feedback	Speaks up and challenges the norm Acknowledges when things don't work and learns Gives and accepts constructive feedback
	Integrity by advocating and applying high ethical standards every day	Operates with high ethical standards Is humble, caring, shows trust, respect and empathy Lives by the code of conduct even when facing resistance or difficulties

U NOVARTIS

Figure 3. Novartis revised Leadership Framework 2015.

The emphasis on culture as a shared platform for professional interaction creates a sense of mutual understanding and belonging. In practice it provides the opportunity to create a professional working environment that builds on a single cohesive, purposeful model, despite the many different nationalities, styles, approaches and businesses within Novartis.

Stefanie and other executive informants described how they had to take time to build the capacity to work in a new environment. Many used Executive Coaches and internal training programmes to work on their *'self and style in relation to others'*, and also built resilience and emotional intelligence to deal with the new environment. How different is it really to work in other locations and how can mobility serve as a Leadership tool? According to the

Harvard Business Review article, '5 Ways to Foster a Global Mindset', Leaders must simultaneously work to embed a sense of global thinking into their corporate cultures and into the ways they operate on a daily basis. You want each office to take on its own culture and flavour, but to prevent silos from forming, you will need to ensure that employees truly know what your company stands for and what you believe in, so that everyone is aligned and moving in the same direction (https://hbr.org/2019/07/5-ways-to-foster-a-global-mindset-in-your-company).

ii. Mobile Leaders

Transnational persons are key 'flows' in Castells' (2000) theorisation of the global city in the 'space of flows'. Castells argues that, as the technocratic-financial–managerial elite occupy leading positions of command and control in the world-system, they require specific spatialities (the global cities) to reproduce their cosmopolitan interests and practices. Furthermore, Castells (2000: 446) suggests that elites are 'global' and this globality is reflected in 'personal micro-networks' which are grounded in 'residential and leisure-orientated spaces, which along with the location of headquarters, tend to cluster dominant functions in carefully segregated spaces' (Beaverstock 2002: 525-526). This idea builds on the work on Transnationalism by Glick Schiller, Basch & Szanton-Blanc (1992), which discusses social practices across national boundaries. The fixed versus mobile paradigm, however, always leads to a critique of the tension between belonging and integration (Salazar 2015).

> 'We know it is a difficult system here, we know it is a complex organisation and that there are a lot of processes, but once you figure out how it works, you can make it work for you. It took me around 6 months to understand how this whole thing works ... It's like people are trying to understand you and your position and your thought processes are not that obvious ... and you reflect and understand how people think and why, try to understand their situation, their position, their reasons and attune yourself. That took about a third of my assignment in Basel and then my network grew.'
>
> Rajesh

Looking through the lens of leadership practices that focus on individual Intellectual Capital, I understand the concept of mobility as one of relationships between the self and space. Using soft skills, such as self-awareness and curiosity, to discover how to connect with another individual or another environment is key to leveraging success. In this regard, *Sensorialscapes* can be simply best practices in leading diverse teams with inclusive approaches that the Leader experienced in another geography. Bringing this to headquarters allows sharing expertise to achieve common goals and objectives. As a Leader, Rajesh spent a lot of time building relationships at work in order to be more effective in terms of alignment. He spoke about *'functional alignment, operational alignment and social alignment'* as part of the onboarding process. According to him, an Asian or someone from Latin America (examples of emerging markets) coming to Europe finds it a very *'dry environment'* which takes getting used to. *'It doesn't matter how smart you are, it is the social part … the social part that we give so much importance to in Asia does not have that kind of priority here … I am not saying it is right or wrong, a lot of the time geography decides the thread of the social network.'*

The implications of socialisation in a particular environment need to be understood in order to form meaningful connections and personal or professional networks. It is this cultural understanding that is most developed through mobility. The idea of learning and growing through moving is a strong thread that runs through all my data. Personal choices or circumstances that keep executives on the move and that sustain migration circuits (Lindquist 2008) require a certain degree of strategy to build different kinds of Capital that can be used in the next move. Living in mobility may be challenging but it is a choice: 'staying mobile' (Morokvasic 2004: 11) offers opportunities which are used to advance career trajectories and broaden one's family's lifestyle choices.

My informants were fully aware that they were privileged by their ability to cross borders with ease. Mobility is also a form of Capital, one which Kaufmann et al. (2004) call Motility. Borders are not seen as barriers and this allows an 'ongoing mobility' (Salazar 2015) for the highly skilled, who are able to move without the restrictions placed on other demographic categories. On this basis, Transnationalism and Globalisation flows compose a narrow lens through which to conceptualise a group in constant flux and which views the situation as something 'temporary'. I argue that it is this constant process of change/mobility that actually requires a deeper look at the 'anchors' members of this group carry within themselves.

iii. Success Factors

When it comes to measuring employee performance, companies follow different methods, which often include ratings regarding objectives and goals. This is not a part of my research. However, it came up in my data as a determining factor of mobile Talent Management for both the company and the employee.

> 'When you relocate, especially with family and children, there is one fundamental difference between domestic life and a mobile life. In domestic life [when you are a local], if you lose your job, you will get another job but your ecosystem does not change. In a mobile life, you lose a job and it affects schooling, maybe your location, the things you are used to, everything changes .... Also, you leave to work as a 'talent' and therefore you need to perform. If you are not performing and you get a low rating for 2 consecutive years, you are at risk, your career is dead. You are here because you have something which needs to be continuously encashed because the company has a lot of options, you are not the only one.'
>
> Rajesh

The precarity of international assignments was a constant underlying theme: families were all too aware of the big downside to mobility. Whilst the quality of life may be improved, the tenuous nature of work contracts is ever-present. Rajesh continued: *'When I moved out of India I was product Manager and in 2 years, I was ready to become GM or Country President. Had I stayed, I would not have become that. I completely underestimated my potential and so took a risk. Focus on the opportunities and not the risks.'* As families negotiate the challenges that this uncertainty creates, this awareness becomes, in a way, a strategy for success, a way to 'settle in mobility'

(Morokvasic 2004) and allow the acceleration of career trajectories with a view to maximising relocation opportunities.

> 'My career is going nowhere but my husband's career is important, so when we made our first move 10 years ago, it was a conscious decision that he will go forward and I will be supporting. I never regretted that ... I have told my husband that we can continue this for another 10 years at the most and then it will be time to enjoy in Mumbai ... There is not a single place where I have attached myself. Growing up I moved a lot too and also lived in Dubai for many years. I think my roots are spread all over, where I stayed was home for a time, but Mumbai is where I stayed for the longest time, so in a sense it is home. It has been a romantic life as such and I don't mind this for myself.'
>
> Jaya

During my fieldwork, I heard countless accounts of strategies used to negotiate living in mobility in order to align both career and home. Only recently, a casual conversation with someone at the International School of Basel highlighted the intense stress this lifestyle can involve. A family with three young children moved from Basel to the UK and back to Basel within a six-month period. The Executive took on a role at another company in the UK, moved there with the family, and the children started school there. However, it did not work out at the new company and the decision was made to move back to Basel. I talked with the wife, who said she was *'living in a whirlwind of emotion'* and could not believe that she had been back in Basel for three months already. The last nine months had been spent *' taking care of everyone's stress'* and now it was time for her to plan for herself. She mentioned how she had at first planned to stay in the UK and how she now had to re-think her options to live in Basel again.

Her story was not unique. So many families I know are in flux because of job uncertainty due to companies restructuring, contracts ending, roles changing, etc. Add to that children's schooling and the 'right time to move them', such as after completing a school year, not moving beyond a certain age, finishing high school, etc., and the complexities increase. One mother told me that the youngest of her three children had not experienced a move, so she told her husband that it would be time for them to move once their second child finished high school. It is clear that, despite the tenuous nature of this lifestyle, families are ready and willing to make the necessary adjustments to continue living in 'ongoing mobility' (Salazar 2015). 'Often people think that living abroad is sort of like being on a never-ending holiday. In fact, few things are as difficult as rediscovering our identities in the middle of our adult lives in a community where no one knows us' (Quarck, Resler & Incocciati 2018: page reference). Despite the difficulties, both at work and at home, many professionals and their families clearly desire the experience of *'a European adventure'* (Anne, Spouse).

Building on these reflections, it can be seen that the 'imagined' (Anderson 1983) and often romanticised benefits of a mobile lifestyle far outweigh the cons. Appadurai unpacks the way in which 'imagination' is the source of social practice and agency, and appeals to the self-described 'expat community' which thrives on a certain way of being and then uses the narrative of a *'privileged life'* to compensate for any negative impact. As we have seen, the different actors in this process approach mobility from different perspectives, learning 'about the internal journey we all take when we agree to move abroad. From the moment we make the decision to uproot our lives from the familiar, many things change around us, but more importantly, inside us' (Quarck, Resler & Incocciati 2018: page reference).

> 'I think you need to have a high tolerance for change and I think you need to be able to deal with ambiguity and not know everything. You need to have a thirst for adventure because it is an adventure. It helps to work out where your security is, so where do you get that stability from and how do you maintain that in a new environment.'
>
> Lucy, Executive

iv. Conclusion

The drivers of mobility, as well as understanding the many factors that influence and motivate families to choose this life, are as varied as the people I spoke with. From an HR perspective, companies can become more globally competitive by harnessing diverse talent and leveraging best practices from mobile executives. Companies are constantly evaluating their Talent Management processes in order to better understand their own needs as well as those of their employees. In addition, global competition makes attracting and retaining top talent is a real challenge. As a Trainer, I have been involved in workshops that encourage an Agile Mindset which, in management terms, can be understood as a high form of adaptability to market changes, business practices and customer needs, supported by a flexible and agile organizational structure (agility-definition-innovation-management). Typically, this requires executives to be able to display high levels of agility both in the workplace and at home.

The work practices that focus on personal development to harness business success as a Leader make it clear that a high level of Emotional Intelligence is required to navigate matters such as relocation. 'Only now are the social sciences catching up and coming to grips with those aspects of personality, emotion, cognition and behaviour which were previously judged incapable of being identified, measured and fully understood. Now they're increasingly recognised as crucial to effective functioning, both in the workplace and in our personal lives. Good relationships and coping strategies are key to our success in every area of human activity, from the initial bonding between parent and child to the ability of a manager to bring out the best in his or her employees' (Stein & Howard 2011).

Emotional Intelligence is often produced by setbacks, challenges, ambiguity — all hallmarks of the transient mobile lifestyle, which is why I think it is so highly valued as an important executive skill. What is interesting is that this skill is now intentionally cultivated by both companies and individuals.

Chapter 7 : Basel Topography & Features

'Understanding the local culture' is an oft-used phrase which encapsulates the experience of those who move to Basel. In this chapter, I explore the networks that actors use to negotiate this new space, what experiences they have as they practise daily life and also what strategies they use to feel settled in Basel. I will lay out some of the key features and topography of the city, and examine what negotiations are necessary in 'hardworking Basel, one of Switzerland's richest cities' (http://www.bbc.com/travel/story/20200427-the-swiss-city-where-even-fun-is-serious).

Using Dr Jacques Picard's Cultural Topography diagram (Figure 4; my translation), I note that the cultural spaces in Basel overlap, inform, connect, disconnect and limit experiences for members of the population. Linking this to forms of Capital and Imaginaries affords an additional perspective to the lived experience of people in the city.

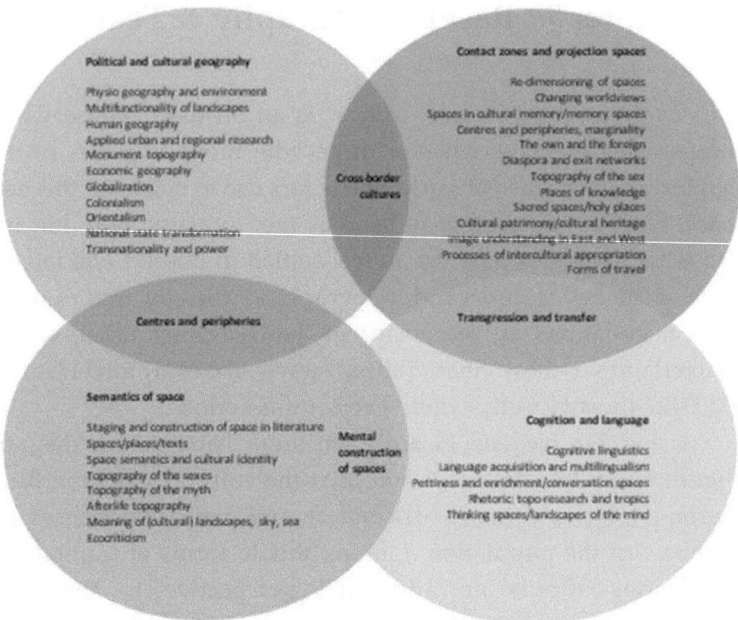

Figure 4 - Scheme 'Cultural Topographies' / University of Basel, Prof. Jacques Picard (2011)

i. Imaginary of Basel

> 'I went to visit my girlfriend at the Novartis Campus for the first time yesterday and I was so surprised! It is so international with people from everywhere — it was like an American city!'
>
> Thomas, Swiss National

Thomas came to visit me at the University to drop off some papers for my husband. We were talking casually about my research topic when he made the above remark. He went on to observe that 'there are a lot of international people in Basel' and that he liked it. His girlfriend enjoys working at the Novartis campus and he has met many new people through her. I asked him for his impressions of how the general public viewed the matter and he said that most people didn't know what was going on 'behind those gates', that it was a 'completely different world' they knew nothing about. 'This "other" must necessarily be understood, however, because it brings an awareness of borders. More precisely, this other beyond a Border constitutes with its difference — marked by a border — the meaning of the object to be understood on this side of the border' (Picard 2016; my translation). In this context, borders constitute the relations or lack of relations between the different social groups.

When I attended a workshop in Lifestyle Migration given by Dr Karen O'Reilly (University of Basel, September 2016), she discussed how privilege shapes migration and also how sometimes the host country's citizens (in this case Swiss nationals) view such migrants as 'residential tourists' who have made Basel their temporary home. This temporary character of home plays a large role in the everyday practices and experiences of both groups. In a way, their privilege renders my research group 'invisible': they are not seen as a 'problem' by the 'hosts', but neither do they fully participate by learning the local language and customs. This liminality manifests in the social relationships as an ambivalent mutual acceptance.

'Imagination is the main source of social practice and agency ... [W]e are functioning in a world that is fundamentally characterised by objects in motion. These objects include ideas and ideologies, people and goods, images and messages, technologies and techniques. This is a world of flows' (Appadurai 1999). These flows invariably influence the Topography, Imaginary and the relationships of individuals to spaces, creating a disjunction of sorts between what is expected and what is possible and, often, what is assumed. Boundaries created through unequal local access can be translated globally and vice versa. In my opinion, the connectivity gained through patterns of consumption reinforces the Imagination, establishing a circularity that creates push and pull factors for mobility.

ii. (Un)common Spaces

'Have you been on a tour of the Novartis campus yet?' asked my informant when I visited her at her office overlooking the Rhine river. She went on to say that I could wander around on my own to look at the architecture since I had a visitor badge. The pride the employees take in the campus was clear every time I visited or talked with someone who worked there. The many restaurants and open-air seating areas onsite are much loved features, along with the diversity of the people. After visiting several Novartis office locations across Europe, I can attest to the unique fraternal aspect of the campus headquarters in Basel. It is unlike anywhere in Basel and this itself creates the sense of a boundary between the local and the international/global. There is a strong security presence at the Novartis campus main gate and everyone who enters has to have their documentation checked and their appointment verified before being issued with a visitor badge.

Once inside, Fabrikstrasse forms an avenue of sorts, on either side of which there are buildings, amenities and green areas. Cyclists and pedestrians account for most of the traffic, but there is also a shuttle bus service that runs between other Novartis locations in Basel. It is a busy campus, particularly during pleasant weather, with lots of people enjoying the outdoor spaces. I conducted several interviews and coaching sessions on a bench overlooking the Rhine iver, or seated at an outdoor restaurant.

Figure 5. Personal sketch of Fabrikstrasse, the main boulevard on Novartis Campus

> 'I mean, we are not a Swiss company, we are an international company and that is just the culture. If you look at any given floor in any building it's not a bunch of Swiss people, it's not a bunch of American people, it's a total cultural mix of people from all over the world, which makes it a very rich experience from a professional perspective. You have the opinions of many different people around with many different backgrounds and perspectives and that's what makes Novartis a rich culture.'
>
> Robert, employee

Looking at the semantics of space in Figure 4, the meaning of being on campus for Novartis employees is manifold. The large open spaces and the feeling of working with a diverse, global mix of people informs the practice of building professional relationships that fosters a culture of collaboration and communication, aimed at reaching a consensus. Robert continued: *'we are, as someone said, a multidimensional matrix because we have to blend strategy with regions and countries and many different dynamics ... it's really just having a mutual respect for each other.'* The campus creates an environment different from the local and simultaneously globally diverse. This construction of space critically taps into the imagination of those who want a global working experience in Basel.

> 'All the buildings are different and unique, I like the diversity of it, that it recognises diversity, recognises difference and yet it all fits together. It is an amazing campus and I feel privileged to work here. There has been a lot of thought that has gone into how well people can collaborate, all the outdoor space, all the different restaurants, getting together for lunch and having discussions over lunch, so it's working.'
>
> Carmen, employee

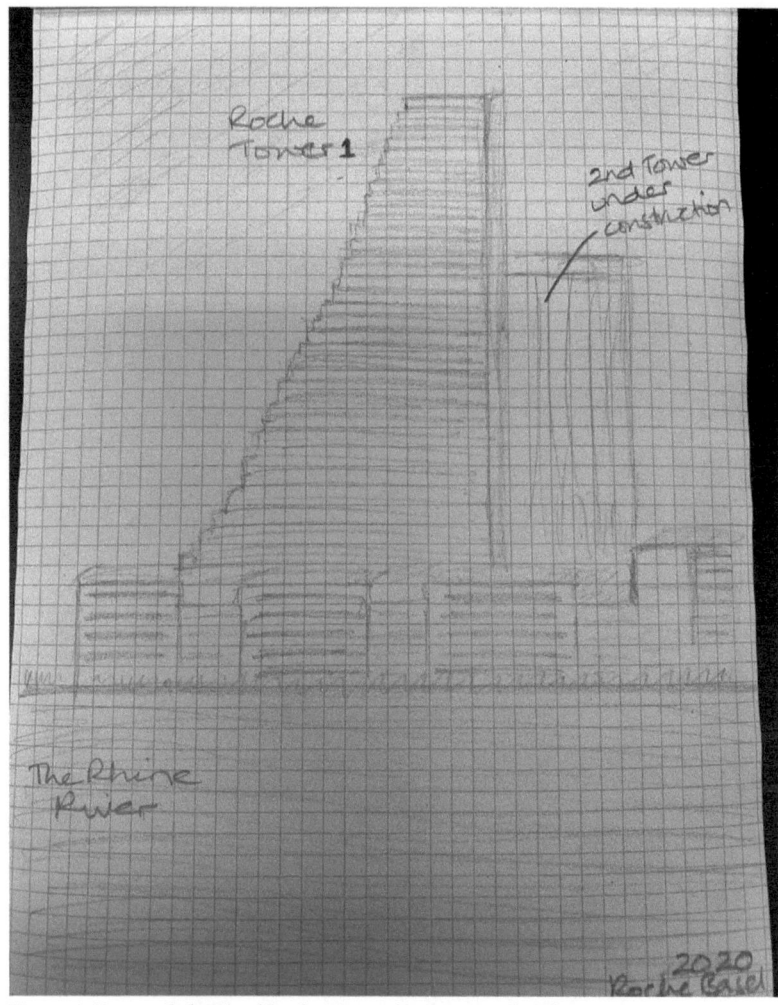

Figure 6. Personal sketch of Roche Tower from across the Rhine river

Figure 7. University of Basel

Figures 6 and 7 depict other spaces I have frequented during this research period and mark key places in Basel. I add them to expand on the topographical dimensions of the city as a leading player in the Pharmaceutical Industrial landscape both locally and globally.

The Roche 178-metre tall Building 1, designed by Herzog & de Meuron, is the tallest building in Switzerland. (Building 2 is currently under construction.) Situated on the Rhine, it is one of the city's landmarks and promises to be 'an office building of the future' built to the 'the highest standards in terms of functionality and technology. Open communication zones on all office levels, extending up to three floors or more, are conducive to open exchanges among employees. The office high-rise offers employees an attractive work environment and top-quality infrastructure. Many colleagues from various areas are relocated to the high-rise. This new physical proximity creates excellent conditions for successful teamwork and the company's innovative force. Building 1 is a most energy-efficient building, i.e. heated with waste heat and cooled with groundwater, while setting new energy efficiency standards with its innovative façade and LED lighting' (https://www.roche.com/basel_building1.htm).

The University of Basel, founded in 1460, is the oldest university in Switzerland and has a history of success going back over 550 years. 'As a comprehensive university offering a wide range of high-quality educational opportunities, the University of Basel attracts students from Switzerland and the entire world, offering them outstanding studying conditions as they work towards their bachelor's, master's or PhD degrees. Today, the University of Basel has around 13,000 students from over a hundred nations, including 2,900 PhD students' (https://www.unibas.ch/en/University/About-University.html). As an academic and scientific community, the university supports the Pharmaceutical Industry by providing research and technical skills, with many student graduates joining Novartis, Roche and other multinational companies based locally.

The university's mission statement is as follows: 'Our goal is to remain one of the best research universities worldwide and to make important contributions to research and social development through scientific knowledge and innovation. As a distinguished university, our innovation derives from the combination of the humanities, social sciences and natural sciences, and close interaction with our public and scientific environment.' In addition it also states: 'Recognizing and fostering diversity and equal opportunities are anchored as guiding principles and integral components of university life. Both within the university and when dealing with our partners, we maintain a culture of dialog, appreciation, respect and tolerance.'

Again, the descriptors point to an international setting within Basel, where the diversity of people and ideas leverage innovation and produce collaborative environments. This picture of a dynamic global environment within Switzerland is part of the lure for mobile individuals and families. "Basel is the most dynamic economic region in Switzerland and one of the most productive and innovative locations worldwide. Basel-Stadt provides employment over 190,000 people from Switzerland and other countries. The economic policy of the Basel government is to create an attractive environment for business and to provide well-directed support for growing companies. In the past few years, the growth posted by the Basel region was well above the average for Switzerland. Liberal employment laws, attractive corporate tax rates, an efficient public administration and political stability are the traditional strong points which benefit companies in the Basel region." (https://www.bs.ch/en/Portrait/economy.html).

iii. Conclusion

In all of the spaces I mentioned above, the striking feature is that it is not necessary to speak German since the business language of English is used and that in and of itself allows for a certain degree of familiarity and comfort for many newcomers. This makes it easier to connect, increases contact zones and blurs the lines between global and local. This allows mobile individuals to participate at some level in society, to operate on the periphery and maybe also form their own sub-community on the margins or, as we can see in the above spaces, within multinational structures in the very centre. Using the Cultural Topography diagram, spaces between the different categories can open up or close down, boundaries can be formed, contact enabled or disabled.

GLOBALLY MOBILE INTELLECTUAL CAPITAL   89

Different forms of Capital, the Imaginary of what Basel holds as a destination are important, but lived experience and practices show elements of Globalisation flows at the helm of local institutions and that makes Basel an attractive choice. Furthermore, the emotions evoked in spaces are critically those that reflect receptivity, innovation, collaboration and inclusion, all necessary features to attract mobile talent. Figure 8 below is of the Frank Gehry-designed building at the Novartis campus and is used in the literature to promote Basel as a world-class destination. 'Media productions exert considerable influence in shaping these imaginaries' (Salazar 2010).

Figure 8
https://www.bs.ch/.imaging/default/dam/bs/en/Portrait/economy/STM0015_Postkarten_OSZE_A6_e_rz_Web1/jcr:content.jpg

Chapter 8: Basel is Unique — City Life

Settling in, familiarising oneself with the basics of recycling, parking, driving, shopping ... the endless list of immediate concerns for newcomers. Basing my research on Globally Mobile Intellectual Capital in Basel was the logical choice for me because upon my arrival I immediately perceived how unique the city was. Building on the Topographical features of the previous chapter, I will explore community spaces frequented by some members of the international community in Basel. In addition, I will continue to explore the evocative nature of what they experienced, expanding on the senses that are engaged.

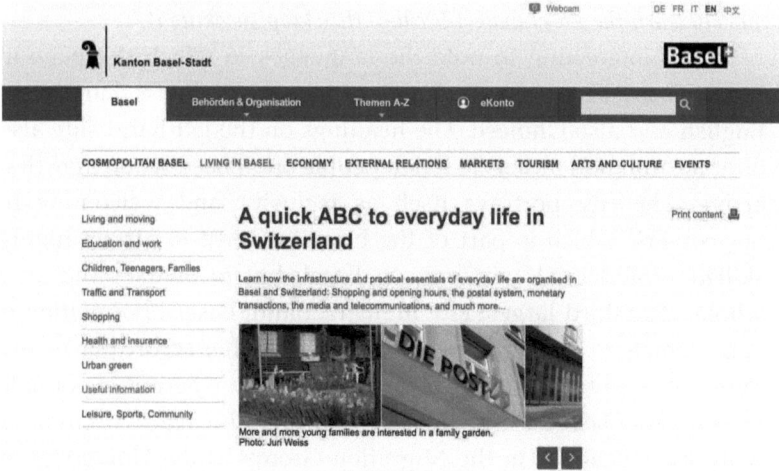

Figure 9. https://www.bs.ch/en/Portrait/living-in-basel/useful-information.html

Basel is divided into two separate cantons: Basel Stadt (Basel City) and Basel Land (Basel Country). Basel Stadt has a population of approximately 200,000 people making it, for most newcomers from abroad, quite a small city. Located close to the borders of France and Germany, with the Rhine river running through it, Basel is able to leverage its geographical location to attract approximately 36,000 cross-border commuters on a daily basis to work in Basel. They contribute to the Swiss workforce but live in either France or

Germany.[2] Special work permits are issued to these daily commuters and it is clear that they form an integral part of the Swiss economy.

> 'I have wonderful colleagues and they really appreciate that I am not a 'Grenzgaenger' (cross-border commuter). When they realised that my address was in Switzerland and that I lived here, they immediately appreciated it.'
>
> Helle, spouse

Helle works as a nurse at a local clinic and recounted her experience with her local colleagues. As a German national, she was able to connect, but *'I spoke my own dialect because I realised the Swiss don't like High German ... they speak their dialect and I had to adjust and quickly learn the Basel dialect because they keep speaking it.'*

It is interesting to note the languages in which the page in Figure 9 can be accessed: three of the official Swiss languages, English and also Chinese. The headings on the left-hand side also offer information on services that people often need when they first arrive. The city portrays itself as inclusive and welcoming to newcomers, which is part of the branding used to attract highly skilled professionals not only to Basel, but to Switzerland as a whole.[3] The third largest city in Switzerland, Basel's population is approximately 30% non-Swiss. This fact alone, according to my informants, gives the city a *'cosmopolitan'* vibe where it is possible to *'survive without learning German'*. Through the many discussions with my colleagues in the Migration Group[4] at the University of

---

[2] My colleagues, Dr Cedric Duchene-Lacroix and Dr Katrin Sontag, have both worked on several papers looking at the multilocal practices of cross-border workers in Basel (e.g. 'The experience of multilocal living – mobile immobilities or immobile mobilities?' in *Bounded Mobilities*).

[3] Two more colleagues, Dr Metka Hercog and Dr Laure Sandoz, authored 'The Mobility of the Highly Skilled Towards Switzerland' (2019), in which they explore the place-branding initiatives supported by Swiss cantons to welcome and retain migrants viewed as valuable by the state.

[4] The Migration Group at the University of Basel was set up by the colleagues mentioned in the previous footnotes as part of a G3S initiative currently run by Dr Julia Buechele, Coordinator of the Graduate School of Social Sciences (G3S). My interactions with this group have given me a good grounding in and knowledge of the many push/pull factors that facilitate the migration

GLOBALLY MOBILE INTELLECTUAL CAPITAL   93

Basel, it became clear to me that the strategies employed by my informants and the companies in my field were part of a larger picture; that is, they fit not only into Basel's image but also into the policies informing Switzerland's economic governance.

Regarding advice, suggestions and tips on life in Basel, there is plenty of information online and lots of Facebook groups can be used to post questions. The page 'Basel International Families', for example, is used by many people I know to connect with other mobile families. Another page is called 'Expats in Basel'. Even basic web searches for information on life in Basel yield plenty of sites containing a wealth of information for newcomers and also for residents keen to explore further. Groups are set up to meet and assist with job searches. There are clubs for hobbies such as hiking, biking, cooking, skiing, etc. Many activities are promoted: outdoor markets, wine tasting, regional food sourcing trips, etc.. Browsing through the web pages, one is left with the impression that there is lots to do in and around Basel.

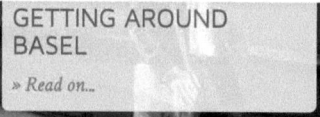

EVERYDAY LIFE IN BASEL

Basel is the third largest city in Switzerland. German is most widely spoken by the native residents, but it is also normal to communicate in English and French. The city is relatively small, easy to get around, and the public transportation options are great. With a large international community, the city is multicultural and is home to people from all around the world. The old city of Basel is one of the best preserved in Europe, with a beautiful atmosphere.

Here you will find all the information you need about living and working in Basel. From cost of living, public transportation, finding a place to live, recycling, childcare and much more – Hello Switzerland is here to help you enjoy your city.

Figure 10 : https://www.helloswitzerland.ch/magazine/living-in-basel

---

process and have also highlighted the importance of discourse in ethnographic research.

i. Reality Bites

According to the abstract of Ulrich Beck's 2008 article, 'The Cosmopolitan Perspective: Sociology of the Second Age of Modernity' (https://doi.org/10.1111/j.1468-4446.2000.00079.x), the '"[s]econd age of modernity" is a magical password that is meant to open the doors to new conceptual landscapes. The whole world of nation sovereignty is fading away – including the "container theory of society" on which most of the sociology of the first age of modernity is based upon [sic].' Beck proposes 'a distinction between "simple globalization" and "reflexive cosmopolitanization".' There is a shift from interconnectedness to living and thinking transnationally, that is, people combine multiple loyalties and identities in their lives.

As my research has shown so far, national groupings are, on the one hand, clear and important and, on the other hand, flexible and seamless. What does this mean in everyday life situations? And how can they be understood?

> 'When I see a post "I am moving from Boston, what should I bring?" I love it! I'm always like,
> God I wish I could get on the phone and tell them exactly what to do! Like, sit down and take note!'
>
> Chloe, spouse

> 'I think, if you're here on your own, that can contribute to unhappiness ... if you're not out there included in some sort of network ... if you're so hung up on the foods that you had at home, the way things were done at home ... some Americans in particular, because I think Europeans transition better to Switzerland than Americans ... depending on the Americans...but if you're used to even ... you know, even in the States in the last [?]huge volume of packaging and etc., etc. ... and the big cars and the big supermarkets and the big trolley ... suddenly all that's gone... and you've a small Migros or a small Coop and ... that's ... that's not everybody's ... uh ... comfort zone and then if you need certain ingredients and you can't find them here, 'cause you're going to the store and everything is written in German ... I mean, a very intelligent friend of mine said she cried in Coop once, 'cause she was looking for something to clean her sink and didn't know where to start [laugh] ... and they are the small things that break you ... now, if you can turn around and laugh at yourself after that ... that's fine. I would just accept

> it ... that it's part of the move ... but if it's you first move .... it's a lot more dramatic.'

Mary, spouse & employee

These two quotations, one of which we have encountered before, are typical of the different perspectives of the Americans and Europeans with whom I interacted. Both groups are very aware of the differences in attitude and are quite comfortable with the stereotypes. The ironic nature of stereotypical behaviour is touched upon as a shared understanding of what it means to be American or British, and the size comparison of houses, fridges, cars, roads on the two sides of the Atlantic is a clear marker of the adjustment process in Basel. I have had many conversations with American friends about buying an extra fridge/freezer for their grocery purchases, furniture not fitting in small living spaces, small uncomfortable sofas, and it quickly became apparent that, for a lot of Americans, the change in materiality brought up many emotions of frustration, regret and nostalgia. This discrepancy between the North American and European lifestyles was omnipresent and was often referred to, particularly by the mobile families of Pharmaceutical Executives. It w very common for families to move back and forth between both continents, adjusting living expectations each time.

What is interesting is that Mary, in her speech, is correct to notice how much more difficult moving is the first time round. She mentions the *'unhappiness'* of being alone to deal with the practical aspects of setting up in a new place, one so different from the US, and how *'intelligence'* is not enough to deal withthe language barrier, for example, or many everyday activities, such as grocery shopping. In her statement, Chloe, having moved abroad from the US for the first time, was quite open about how she struggled at first: *'it is the accompanying spouse who has it the hardest'*. That is what prompted her remark on wanting to help a fellow American and give advice on what to bring when moving to Basel. She was very open with me about the many changes in lifestyle she had to make here and how even the people she interacted with were sometimes not her 'type'. Once again, everyday experiences form an important part of the narrative describing the actors' participation in and interaction with the local environment, with shopping and language being critical factors.

> 'Learn German! Go to a language school and get German lessons. You can start from the bottom. What I really like about the Swiss is that they help you, they appreciate you really wanting to try to speak, that is something they really like. They feel that you want to enter into the community, into the culture that they are really proud of, this is a proud nation, they are proud of what they have achieved, their culture, their rituals during the year in different cantons and when they see someone is really trying, that opens them, you know.'
>
> Helle, spouse

Mary is Irish, Chloe American and Helle German. Mary was a stay-at-home spouse until her children were older and she started working. This was Chloe's first move abroad. Helle lived in the US for nearly ten years before moving here. Their narratives reflect the typical experiences and stories shared on a regular basis in my fieldsite. We touched on different details: how the slanted roofs here make it even more difficult to accommodate bigger furniture, how the lack of preservatives means that you have to go grocery shopping more often in Basel ... numerous differences which affect daily life. The stories recounted above may appear superficial, but they belong to families who also cope with births, deaths, weddings, divorces and graduations, sometimes close by and oftentimes far away. The reality of those moments is never far from my informants' minds. This precarity underlies the so-called 'expat experience'.

> 'So I think we sometimes underestimate the stress of moving and the fact is that people, they need to have information, they need to know what's going to happen, what kind of things do I need, and you don't know what you don't know, you don't know what questions to ask because every time you move it's something different and honestly, even moving here versus moving to Nyon is different.'
>
> Lucy, employee

ii. International School Bubble

A large part of my interactions and participant observation took place at the International School of Basel Region AG (ISB). Many of the Executives in my research group send their children to this school and it is also where my children go to study. I participated in many focus group discussions dealing with the transition of mobile families and Third Culture Kids (TCKs) at the school. This is a topic that feeds into everybody's narratives and highlights the choices, motivations and difficulties of lived experiences abroad. As with many international schools, the transient nature of the community, with lots of arrivals and departures of people throughout the year, requires seeing mobility as an ongoing process. It is something that the children learn to deal with through their many transitory friendships and, as a school community, the ISB offers a lot of support to newcomers as well as to those leaving.

The ISB offers the three International Baccalaureate (IB) programmes for children between the ages of 3-19 years. The IB is renowned for its philosophy of striving 'to develop students who will build a better world through intercultural understanding and respect. IB programmes incorporate quality practice from national and international research and the IB global community. They encourage students to be internationally-minded, within a complex and hyper-connected world' (https://www.ibo.org/).

WELCOME TO ISB

> The only not-for-profit, English language, three programme International Baccalaureate (IB) World School in the region.

THE ISB
Difference

Figure 11 https://www.isbasel.ch

Figure 11 is taken from the homepage of the ISB website. The fact that it provides a quality IB education for children between the ages of 3 and 19 is a huge draw for families moving to Basel. It feeds into aspirations of being 'globally minded' and 'cosmopolitan' and of broadening the children's experiences and perspectives.

> 'So I thought about it and yeah, you could do anything for 3 years and if it helps the kids get a leg up for college, help mould them into global human beings, have this opportunity ... I think the school plays a big part in the well-being of the kids fitting in, ISB is great'
>
> Chloe, spouse

Parents are encouraged to become involved in the ISB community by participating in many social events as well as by supporting classroom activities – listening to students read, practise mathematics or cooking – and other learning situations that require extra support.

A VIBRANT AND ENGAGED SCHOOL COMMUNITY

ISB strongly welcomes parent involvement and participation. Parent support plays a vital role in creating a successful and happy school environment.

Studies have proven that strong parental involvement is directly linked to student achievement and success. On our campuses, we have observed this connection on a more personal level. Parent participation generally enables students to learn more, as well as to contribute to our affirmative learning environment – both of which are crucial in the fulfillment of our school Mission.

| ABOUT | WELCOME PROGRAMME | MUSIC & SPORTS BOOSTERS | LEARNING SUPPORT PARENTS | AISB |

There is no better way to learn about the school, make new friends and contribute at the same time!

Run by parent volunteers, the ISB Community Association (CA) is committed to building a strong school spirit by:

- supporting efforts to increase knowledge about the school
- promoting cultural awareness by celebrating diversity
- cultivating social interaction and positive attitudes to make all feel welcome

Many activities take place throughout the year such as the Back to School BBQ. The International Festival and Quiz Night are fund-raising events where all families are encouraged to participate. The funds are used to benefit the school community by sponsoring programmes and purchasing special equipment. Community members are invited to attend CA meetings to share ideas and get involved in planning future events.

Figure 12 https://www.isbasel.ch

Figure 12 gives a sense of the kind of community networks that can be built through the school. There is a Welcome Programme 'creating a hospitable environment for new and returning families. This community group represents many cultures and year levels and reflects the international, inclusive nature of ISB. Through a host of relaxed and enjoyable opportunities organized throughout the year – such as day trips, coffee gatherings and receptions – they reach out to families to ease their transition and create opportunities for greater interaction and communication within the school community.'

iii. (In)Visible Boundaries

There is a strong community feeling amongst ISB families. Deep friendships are built as a result of relying on each other for social activities or for helping during an illness, providing child or pet care, plus regular daily activities such as shopping, sports, etc. This network is encouraged by the school and provides an unchallenged comfort zone for many people. There are 'country coffees' held throughout the year based on nationality, so the Americans will have one, as will the Spaniards, the Portuguese, the Indians, the British, etc., allowing parents to get in touch with people who speak the same language, come from the same country/culture, etc. This is often the first group of people that one meets at the school and invariably forms the core network.

> 'I feel like you kind of align by country ... yeah, the Brits, Americans kind of hang and so I've broken a couple of barriers, I'm with some Dutch but only because I play tennis, but for the most part it's by country. I think it's normal because you just want to be reminded of your home country ... like, you know, the dynamic. The kids are able to diversify more easily at school, my daughter has an Indian friend.'

Chloe, spouse

Building on 'imagination as social practice' (Appadurai 1996), and the emotions tied to this 'world', my informants are cognisant of the connectors needed to establish themselves. They seek out the familiar in order to cope with the new, understanding the limitations this may pose.

> 'I mean, it's not like I am picky but I definitely have certain types of friends and here it's probably people I wouldn't even like ... I'm kind of mad at myself because I feel like there are people I would've written off but I don't have a ton of options at this point, like I am limited to my country and Brits.'

Chloe, spouse

Chloe and many of the parents I spoke to at the school had similar experiences of imagining a 'global experience', coming and finding comfort with a familiar social group and then feeling constrained because they were not *'experiencing other cultures'*. The aspiration of becoming 'cosmopolitan' through an international assignment is a strong motivator for many. Very often it is those, like Chloe, on their first move abroad who struggle with stepping outside their comfort zone to create new networks. Discussing this with the Welcome Committee Chair, the feedback they received is that whilst it is true that they are reproducing cultural boundaries, for many newcomers, particularly those who are first timers or who may not speak English very well, the ability to establish ties within one's own cultural community is often a *'lifesaver'*. The next step, that of connecting with other nationalities, is theirs to take when they are ready.

iv. Consuming Cosmopolitanism

My respondents often framed their mobile experience as one of gaining knowledge of other cultures. This fed into the narrative of the mobile imaginary lifestyle of exposing oneself to the foods, traditions, languages, people, etc., of different backgrounds and cultures in order to become *'globally minded'*. 'The perspective of the cosmopolitan must entail relationships to a plurality of cultures' (Hannerz 1990: 239). Seeking and practising these relationships through consumption of the Other in their daily lives is what many of my informants experienced here in Basel. It was simultaneously exciting and exhausting, fulfilling and frustrating, easy and difficult: a process of constant negotiation.

'Today's cosmopolitans combine experience of various media with various forms of experience — cinema, video, restaurants, spectator sports and tourism, to name just a few — that have different national and transnational genealogies' (Appadurai 1996: page reference). The cultural capital built up by my research group was accumulated sometimes through design and oftentimes through despair. *Sensorialscapes* created through food, for example, allow a connection through eating to the memory of past moments of eating that particular food, with certain people, at a certain time. This 'cultural shaping of the senses' (Korsmeyer & Sutton 2011, which includes memory as a sense, allows a deeper understanding of how we experience food socially. Both memory and the senses are categories that help us shape our perceptions of the world. This constant process of (re)creating identity through eating particular foods and then being cosmopolitan by 'trying different foods' is problematic for some and a badge of openness for others.

> 'There is a big American get-together around the Thanksgiving holiday, that's great, celebrating your culture, but our goal to be here in this multicultura placel, even if there are elements we don't care for, is to be open to the culture, to where you are, to what it is. There are things you like and things you don't like and that's what you learn from. And you may or may

not reach a point in your second or third mobile tour that you decide that you are done or really love immersing yourself in other cultures.'

Robert, employee

v. Conclusion

An intentional approach to mobility and accepting the discomfort of adapting to different norms is a common thread that runs through my data. Cultural cosmopolitanism is much sought after and valued. As discussed in previous chapters, it is also a much valued Leadership skill. A stint in Basel is viewed as an opportunity to develop both personally and professionally, despite any perceived difficulties. The opportunity to travel within Europe and explore new sensorial experiences are additional value propositions.

Navigating the local in Basel requires a degree of flexibility that accepts ambiguity: not understanding the tram announcements despite having learnt basic German, because they are in the local dialect, being OK with not knowing your neighbours very well, making friends who will move on to countries you may never visit, maintaining close ties with family and friends living in distant lands ... The list is potentially endless and requires managing emotions and using self-awareness to balance oneself in order to make sense of all the adjustments.

The mixture of boundaries between cultures and identities sometimes allows the nation to persist; at other times, however, it encourages the dynamics of Capital consumption and the boundaries blur a little. The ambivalence of both states is, in my opinion, a process lying on a continuum running from the hold of the nation state to a more globalised, interconnected, cosmopolitan outlook. I use these terms knowing that they mean different things to different people; however, the ability to intentionally leverage and negotiate spaces on the basis of effective emotions and strategies to facilitate mobility is something that I have witnessed in my research. It forms a part of Intellectual Capital.

Chapter 9: Mobility or Not?

The title of my research refers to the Intellectual Capital of skills and experiences built up by individuals as they progress in their careers. I have argued that this involves not only hard technical professional skills but also Leadership traits that have been built over time. If we consider Talent and Mobility, we notice that there is a clear assumption that Talent cannot succeed without Mobility. What does that mean? In this chapter I focus on case studies of informants who challenged this assumption.

In my view, Mobility as a concept provides a flexibility of approach that the term 'Migration' does not. Passing through the various Migration Group discourses since my arrival at the University of Basel, it became clear to me that Mobility seemed more 'positive' and Migration 'negative'. These value judgements reflected the view in my field that the choice 'to become mobile' was not only career enhancing but also a lifestyle initiative. I wanted to allow my informants to 'self describe' and articulate their journeys. 'An Anthropological approach to mobility and migration starts with the questions of how migratory movements are experienced by the people who are studied and how concepts are constructed in this context rather than letting a predefined conceptual setting determine the analysis' (Camenisch & Mueller 2017).

When focusing on movement, the construction of migration and mobility is dynamic, making the two terms complementary, framing the discourse as a complex relationship that can produce multiple outcomes. In effect, as with the subject of my research, movement can be leveraged to (re)produce lifestyle or business results. Mobility is often associated with success and, as I have noted, it is often constructed by actors to exemplify this.

Brian had moved to Basel with his young wife and baby daughter from the US six months prior to our meeting. He had worked for Novartis on the East Coast and had enjoyed a successful career. He was very frank about the difficulties he was facing here in Basel during our wide-ranging interview. While in the US, he had been working quite closely with the team at Basel HQ and did not understand why he had to physically move.

> 'I had many difficult conversations with my Manager about why I had to move. It makes no sense to me that this is a box-ticking exercise which has made me and my family miserable.'

In the US, Brian lived in a big, lovely suburban home close to his parents and had a strong network of childhood friends who also lived close by. His wife had grown up in similar circumstances and was very connected to her friends and family in the US. They used to go sailing at the weekends, had easy access to childcare, extra help, etc. Basically, there were very well settled at home. He said that he felt that he had no choice but to move to Basel for his 'promotion' and that it really made no sense to him because he had been working well remotely.

The family found it very hard to settle in Basel. The language, a smaller home, no trusted childcare, nothing to do on the weekends, particularly Sundays, healthcare, a *'very strange and conservative/rigid'* atmosphere, unhappiness at work ... They had really struggled and decided to cut their stay short and move back home to the US. Brian had to push very hard to convince his Manager that he was not ready to stay for the full duration of his contract, that he was unable to adjust to the lifestyle and was actually unwilling to do so. There was no need for him to compromise and, fortunately for him, his Manager agreed to let him continue his role from the US.

In this case, due to Brian's specific skill set, an exception was made to allow him to move back to the US and continue his role there. As an outlier, someone who did not enjoy the international assignment experience, he was frustrated by the focus on mobility as a stepping stone to promotion and future career success. Both the employee and the spouse felt the vulnerability required to be open and challenge the norm . Whilst my field of informants fall into an elite socio-economic bracket, this human dimension leads to the idea of mobility as something not seamless or indeed frictionless. What I discovered was that companies need to demonstrate more and more flexibility in order to retain talent as more and more executives negotiate what works best for them and their families. This tangential awareness is reflected in organisational development strategies, where, as one Roche HR partner stated, *'we need to be cognisant of the impact that change has on people; maybe not everyone is made for it. If there are untenable circumstances, we need to find a way in partnership with the individual and organisation. It needs to make sense, of course.'"*

i. Dual Career Choices

I first met Tracy in the corridor outside our youngest childrens' classroom. Both she and her husband were working full time and had just moved to Basel from the US. They had four children between the ages of 4 and 10 years and had recently found someone to help them with afternoon pick-ups, after school activities and childcare.

> 'Child care is just so expensive over here! I can't believe how much I pay for a few hours of work every afternoon! We are stuck in a tiny apartment in town and I am going crazy! The company doesn't think about what happens to families when they move us. If my husband and I don't get transferred back to the US soon then we will be heading for divorce because it's so stressful!'

As I got to know Tracy better, it became clear that most of her work was still in the US, so she had to travel back quite a lot. Her husband's work, however, was mostly at headquarters in Basel. They had thought that they would move to Basel and try to make it work but the lack of support on the personal front made it very challenging. Tracy and the children eventually moved back and her husband continued his role in Basel, travelling back to the US as much as possible.

The decision-making process for dual career families differs from family to family. Very often, one spouse decides to take a 'back seat' for the sake of the move and then looks for opportunities once settled. For Tracy and her husband, it was clear from the outset that they would both continue with their demanding roles. However, the pressure of juggling family life with two careers in a new place proved in time not to be worth it. The strain on the couple was too much and so they decided it would be best for the family to be back in their old, familiar, supportive, US network and have the husband travel to Basel when needed. Initially, like most families, the lure of a stint in Europe was exciting and welcomed as an opportunity to travel.

ii. Support Networks

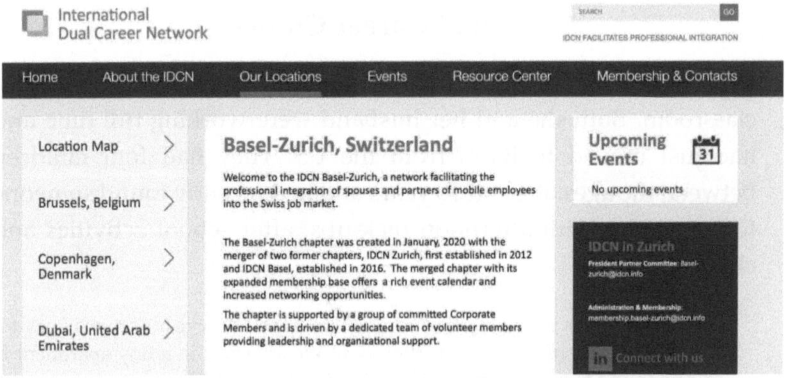

Figure 13. http://www.idcn.info/our-locations/basel-zurich-switzerland.aspx

This challenging work dynamic is not unusual for dual career couples and, as the above website indicates, companies are keenly aware of the issues at work. What is interesting to note, however, is that this group (along with many others like it) is run by volunteers and therefore occupies a grey area where accountability is concerned. The onus is on the individual/spouse to seek out and use the resources on hand in order to optimise their situation. There are plenty of Facebook groups and other MeetUp groups that cater to various demographics, providing plenty of opportunities for people to connect. Social media is full of networking groups, classes, courses, workshops; in fact, there seems to be a real need to showcase the many events and activities open to English-speakers in Basel. I have found that this tendency has only increased during my stay here but, unfortunately, cannot explore it further as it lies outside of my research focus.

Going back to the International Dual Career Network (IDCN), Figure 14 is a screen-grab from the website, but could just as easily come from any of the groups targeting an English-speaking audience. The focus is on catering to people from diverse backgrounds — in this case to meet recruiters — but actually it is to connect mobile people who will share their experiences and create networks in Basel.

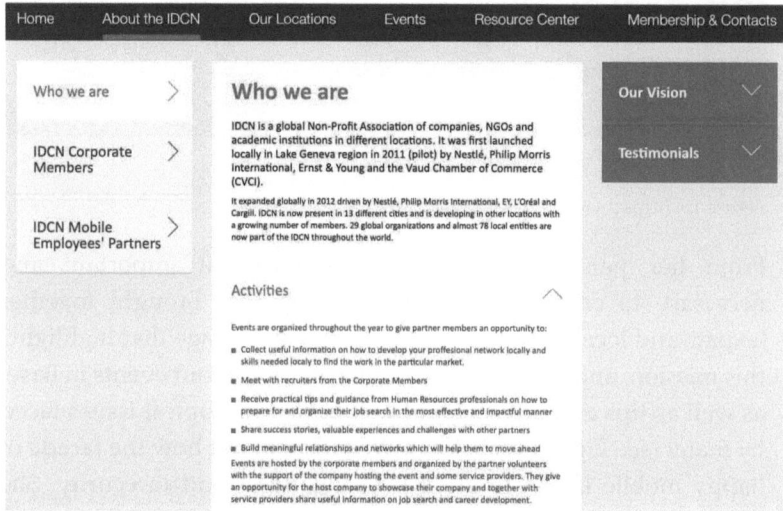

Figure 14: http://www.idcn.info/about-the-idcn/who-we-are.aspx

> 'My ex didn't want to move because she also had her professional career and we compromised for some time with me commuting for nearly 2 years. We had no kids and it was a good compromise. I became tired and wanted to move here but she did not come with me. I moved here alone.'
>
> Carlos, employee

I first met Kathy Hartmann-Campbell at an event for the Professional Women's Group in Basel (https://www.pwg-basel.ch/) and soon learned that she was also a Coach, had her own business and was the founder of Basel Connect. Originally from the US, Kathy met and married a Swiss man and went through what she called 'culture shock' after moving to Basel in 1982.

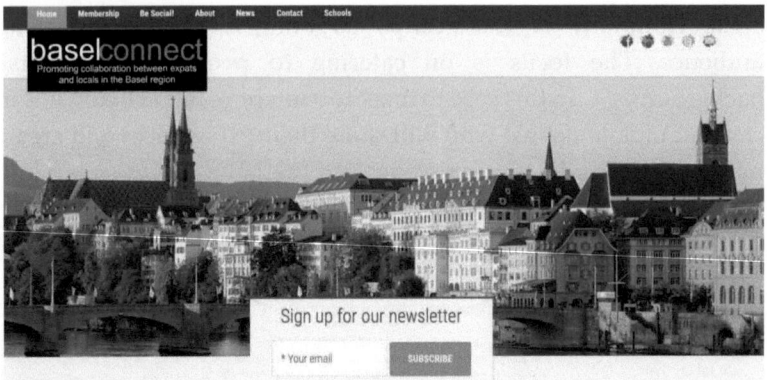

Figure 15: https://www.baselconnect.com/

From her personal experience, she found it important and necessary to create a networking group that brought together 'expats and locals'. Figure 15 depicts the main page that highlights this mission, and the site is full of information about events in Basel as well as tips and advice on how to deal with topical issues faced by many (see Figure 16, below). We talked about how the facade of happy mobile lives can often hide loneliness and insecurity. She mentioned that she had many clients and personal friends who maybe drank too much alcohol trying to deal with the anxiety they were feeling. That she had seen many family separations during her many years here and how she felt it was important to also talk about the difficulties of the 'expat life'.

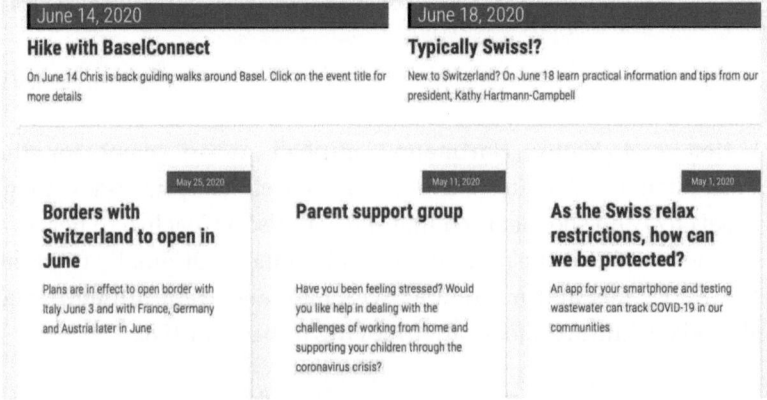

Figure 16 : https://www.baselconnect.com/

iii. Conclusion

Brian's story is not unusual. In fact, over the years, it has become very clear to me that there are numerous 'costs' and considerations that factor into choosing mobility both at the personal and professional level. Companies pay a lot of attention to managing talent and the importance of mobility as a part of a leadership career trajectory has been contested. Through the many discussions, workshops, interviews and observations, the 'value' that is attached to a mobile lifestyle has become clear to me.

Corporate Executives, and their families, who relocate for work assignments are viewed as 'valuable assets', 'high potentials', 'mobile talent'. 'International assignments constitute a proven method for developing global managers. Most Senior managers have extensive international experience ... Indeed, expatriation allows junior managers or high-potential employees to face new situations, to develop new competencies, especially when it comes to acting autonomously and taking risks, thus facilitating the development of abilities required for becoming a senior manager' (Waxin 2007).

What about their spouses? What about their families? Carlos had to decide between his fiancée and his career. Because they did not have kids, he chose his career. Brian was fortunate enough to be able to convince his company that he could be an effective leader despite cutting his international assignment short. Tracy moved back with her children to provide the stability she needed for her family so that she could continue with her job; her husband took on the international commuter role to make it work. Once again, the emotional toll is important.

The assumption that this is a family decision feeds into the structures that are in place to facilitate corporate jobs. Spouses are afforded support but, in effect, it is really up to the individual to find out more and make use of the available options. It is often not easy to 'transfer skills' from one country to another because of varying qualifications and local employment laws. In Basel, despite the many support networks catering to personal and professional support, the unique and variable nature of each and every case requires a flexible approach by all the stakeholders. People almost automatically link horizontal or geographical mobility with vertical-economic (financial), social (status), and Cultural (cosmopolitan) 'climbing'. In sum, mobility entails much more than mere movement; it is infused with meaning (Frello 2008; Greenblatt 2009). Moreover, mobility 'means different things, to different people, in differing social circumstances' (Adey 2006: 83)

Chapter 10 : Swiss Spaces

Countries shape their migration policies on according to multiple factors and Europe in particular has had to contend with the effects of nearby geopolitical situations. My colleagues Dr Metka Hercog and Dr Laure Sandoz[5] have researched some of the structures that support push and pull factors in Switzerland by looking at migrant eligibility, visa quotas, work permits, etc., to determine who is categorised as 'welcome' and 'highly skilled'. There is a clear need and dependence on migrants as 'agents of development'. In this chapter, I will explore some of the dynamics that have struck me as interesting and that played a role in my participants' experiences.

i.   Gruezi! Greetings!

Figure 17: © Carlo Schneider

---

[5]   https://kulturwissenschaft.philhist.unibas.ch/de/forschung/mobilitaet/ & https://nccr-onthemove.ch/

The above cartoon by Carlos Schneider was brought to my attention during a discussion with my students in a class on Migration and Mobility. They said that 'integration' should not be treated as occuring in only one direction — from the 'migrants' — but should be something that the hosts (country/place/nationals) engage in, that integration went 'both ways'. Agreeing, I extended the idea by saying that relationships require a two-way process for success, stability and overall engagement through the understanding of different perspectives. Government policy often imposes requirements but the 'experience' of such imposed power dynamics is not uniform, and plays out with significant disparity and ambivalence in society. I was curious to know where this cartoon came from and I was also aware that my interaction was with a group of Changing Societies Masters[6] students at the University of Basel, whose views were perhaps not indicative of a wider change in society.

Later on the same day, when I was coaching a client, an American, he spoke of how 'ineffective' he felt in a German environment. He felt 'alienated' and 'unsure'; there was a 'boundary' he wasn't able to cross. He is married to a bilingual woman (whose mother is German) who wants to remain in Basel for the children to connect with their Germanic roots. He speaks 'broken German' and needs to pass the Common European Framework of Reference for Languages (CEFR) A1 level (https://www.coe.int/en/web/common-european-framework-reference-languages/level-descriptions) exam in order to fulfil his Swiss residency requirements. This created a lot of anxiety for him despite working really hard on learning German and being able to converse in the language. In fact, one of his goals in working with me was to force some accountability so that he would take the A1 German exam, which he had been avoiding for some time.

If we examine the importance of language as a 'connector', it is clear that it is used to articulate experiences and, within a culture,

---

[6] I co-taught Critical Perspectives on Migration and Mobility as part of the Masters in Changing Societies Programme at the University of Basel (https://dgw.philhist.unibas.ch/en/ma-changing-societies/).

those experiences and their nuances are shared, understood and contain a certain meaning. That is why it is commonly regarded as difficult to translate a meaning exactly from one language to another, and there is of course an innate connection between culture and language which people infer to be part of 'stereotypical behaviour/group thought'. The scope of my dissertation, however, does not allow for further analysis of this topic. Since my interest is in the 'experience' of my informants, the relevant factor is the institutional framework in Switzerland that pushes for German language acquisition and, in particular, the discomfort that not knowing German provokes in my informants.

ii. Permission, Please!

In the 1970s, Switzerland adopted a quota system to regulate immigration numbers and, according to official statistics, only 4.1% of long-term immigrants in Switzerland in 2015 met the quotas (SEM 2016). At the Cantonal level, Basel Stadt 'regularly receives four to six times more permits than officially allocated to it' (Sandoz 2018) and has to rely on Federal support to provide permits. It is clear that the pharmaceutical companies in Basel far exceed their limit. What I am curious about is the leniency that may be afforded to 'highly skilled workers' when it comes to their German language proficiency. This is a question that I could not fully investigate, but I do know of countless cases where employees and their spouses have not engaged in learning German for various reasons: 3-year stays, the difficulty, the feeling that there is '*no real need, you can get on without it!*'

The reasons for not learning German often come up in casual conversations and, just recently, I was unofficially told that companies often seek exemptions for those who do not achieve even the minimum level of language competence required by the Cantonal authorities for permit renewal. This goes against the strict rules and regulations applied to those who do not have the support of a large multinational organisation. Another 'grey zone' which manifests flexibility and ambivalence. Indeed, many of my informants did not make use of their company's language assistance stipend or else passed it on to their spouse, who would use it to start German language classes but eventually give up.

> 'So I just started but I don't have lots of time and it's interesting that probably my admin is protecting me because it's horribly busy right now and I haven't had a lesson for a while and, to be honest, I don't use it at all. I mean it's English at work, but learning German or Swiss isn't that helpful to me, I can live without it. I actually like Basel, it's much more international than Nyon, that's for sure, apart from the fact that I don't know what anybody is saying and I find it hard because I take the tram and when they say something or it is written I literally have no idea what's going on, so that's difficult but it's an easy city to be in.'
>
> Lucy, employee

During her stay in Basel, like many people I interviewed, Lucy did not feel the need to learn much German and, although she started classes, she did not continue with them despite the discomfort she felt when using public transport. *'It's frustrating when they are trying to say something to me but, to be honest, most people speak English and help when I say I am trying to learn. I can say my name and where I am from.'* As a form of Capital, learning the language is useful to eliminate a certain degree of discomfort when interacting with the local environment and to build new relationships in the community. 'The main challenges concern: life in a foreign language (at a practical and relational level), the quality of their social relationships and a feeling of deskilling linked either to problems in accessing the labor market or to the contrast between their high performance on the work level and their lack of autonomy on a social/practical level' (Nunes-Reichel & Santiago-Delefosse 2015).

Anecdotal evidence supports the idea that the decision to learn German in Basel is based on whether it is officially required or not, specifically when it comes to residence permits. If companies are able to renew permits without the official language requirements, then people are not inclined to subject themselves to the rigorous learning process. If language certification is required, then the tests are taken to get the permit. There is of course a small number of people who wish to use the opportunity to immerse themselves in a new language and culture, but they often decide to stay beyond their initial international assignment contract.

iii. Integration Means?

'Integration means collaboration and coming together'

Prof. Walter Leimgruber

The cartoon depicted in Figure 17 prompted me to dig deeper into its origins and this led me right back to my department at the University of Basel! I met with Prof. Walter Leimgruber, one of my PhD supervisors, in his capacity as President of the Federal Commission on Migration (EKM) (https://www.ekm.admin.ch/ekm/en/home.html), to find out more about the Swiss perspective regarding the non-Swiss population. We had an illuminating discussion on the commission's mandate, research and efforts to promote what I see as a recognition of the contribution that all members of a society make regardless of their origin. As the English-language homepage shown in Figure 18 states, the mandate is 'to address social, economic, cultural, political, demographic and legal issues that arise from the residence of foreign nationals in Switzerland. The subject areas covered range from refugee protection and economic migration to social cohesion and transnational issues.'

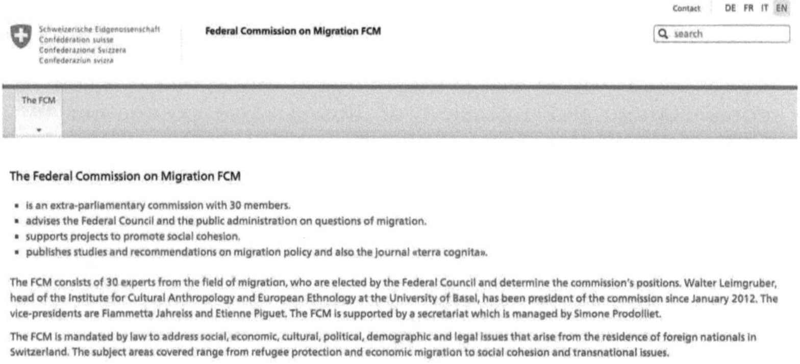

Figure 18 : https://www.ekm.admin.ch/ekm/en/home.html

The complex nature of this mandate is not lost on an anthropologist of Leimgruber's stature. The inclusion of different actors and voices in the commision was impressive and left me feeling hopeful of a new, more inclusive way forward. The commission's latest project, 'Neue Wir' (New We), focuses on expanding the story of society to 'everyone who lives here' (Wir) instead of constraining it to Us vs the Other.

The very nature of a society and the way that it is governed, particularly when it comes to dealing with multicultural issues, is complex. It requires what I feel is an understanding by all concerned of the necessary relationships that build cohesion through empathy, which enables one to develop a capacity to imagine other perspectives. I was impressed by the work that Swiss government commissions do and it was clear from my discussions with Walter that ideas continue to evolve and there is a push for change over time. I did, however, note that neither international families nor individuals were represented; and, whilst I can understand the reasoning behind this, I do believe that the group in Switzerland is large enough to warrant consideration. I am aware of certain international associations that liaise with government authorities, but such connections seems to informal. In addition, multinational companies are represented in business channels, and this means that the social impact of their employees is often overlooked.

Similarly, when it comes to bi-national marriages or even Swiss citizens with dual citizenship, the numbers are quite high for a small country like Switzerland. The discourse around the representation and inclusion of this diverse population in a democracy, particularly in Switzerland, is important to encourage civic engagement. All of these reflections and considerations are interesting, but not part of my investigation. I acknowledge them as important factors that play a part in the lives of those who live here in Basel; as influencing discourses that shape policy and society; as what make Basel a unique part of the country.

iv. Conclusion

Exploring the migration policies that shape push and pull factors in Switzerland raises the problematic concept of Integration, which can be loosely defined as 'understanding the language and codes of everyday life in a given place'. This means displaying a certain degree of familiarity in everyday interactions with people and spaces; showing an understanding of the 'unwritten cultural rules & norms'. Beyond this relational aspect of Integration, I am again compelled to look at the sensorial aspect to understand the relational connections and limitations of what 'feels familiar'. The emotions underlying empathy can be the anchors for a *Sensorialscape* that offers an embodied experience for individuals to negotiate belonging.

EKM demonstrates that opening up societal space through inclusive dialogue plays a role in shaping and defining next steps in government policy. It may be slow but it is effective.

Chapter 11: Exploring 'I'

In this chapter, I include my personal journey in the narrative as a way to add context and a degree of reflexivity to the dissertation. I moved to Basel with my husband and three daughters from Dubai in August of 2014. My husband took on a role as part of an international assignment with his logistics company, which had offices in Basel and Zug. This was our first stint in Europe as a family after living in Hong Kong and Dubai, where I left my job as a Lecturer of Global Awareness at Zayed University. As a native in this field, I share my experience of getting to know Basel.

As an anthropologist who studying phenomena that include aspects of my lived experience, reflexivity for me is essentially a process that entails the interaction of various subjectivities (Briggs 1970; Geertz 1972; Rabinow 1977). Being reflexive enables researchers to critically consider their own cultural biases and negotiate various ways of seeing while investigating and 'translating' culture(s) (Geertz 1971). Self-identifying with the group that I was studying allowed many of my informants to open up and reassured them that I would 'get' what they were talking about. 'How can someone who has never moved really understand what it means?' This was a common refrain in this mobile community. In addition, my status reduced the reluctance to share and problematise what is often viewed as a privileged way of life. Relocation, with its many variables, is a process marked by emotionality. A shared experience allows an empathic connection that crosses the traditional markers of nationality, ethnicity, gender, etc., and is something that brings the international community in Basel together. Mobility as a way of life is the intersectionality of this group and relegates many other factors to the periphery. 'As migrants move from one place to another, they also destabilise fixed borders and boundaries, whether geographic or inter-categorical' (Bastia 2014: page reference).

Cultural representation and the negotiation of identity, along with the complexity inherent to translating another individual's experience, are fraught with ambiguity. However, to me, each person's subjectivity was legitimate and their narrative added to my research framework. The matter of positionality did not come up much during my interviews, unless my informant was curious to know more about me. It was neither discounted nor highlighted, and when it arose I did not feel that it was counterproductive. Daily informal conversations with parents at the ISB, along with casual interactions with colleagues and friends, allowed the snowballing of information and informants, My immersion in the field was complete on many levels and from multiple perspectives.

My presence as an anthropologist was fully acknowledged at every step and thus the critical legitimacy of my study involved a reflexive process of questioning my biases and assumptions at every stage, and of clearly articulating them whilst engaging in data collection such as interviews and participant observation. This self-reckoning provoked moments of self-doubt, which for me was part and parcel of the process. Accepting my positionality allowed access to open dialogue, critical exchanges, academic rigour and the opportunity to frame my positionality in objective terms. Did I ever feel like an outsider? Yes, of course. Particularly when I was in curious, questioning, research mode, when constructing my field and my position in it. The process was fluid, as were the boundaries.

'Although the native and researcher look alike, speak the same language and share many of the same beliefs and customs, the researcher still approaches the natives to observe them' (Nelson 1996). Nelson goes on to postulate that the constant negotiation of multiple allegiances, accountabilities and perspectives is par for the course, as I came to realise. It can be seen adding significance through rapport, insights and easy access. I came to see it as being as much of an enabler as a disabler, the key being a readiness to articulate and negotiate positionality when it came up.

Understanding that ethnographic fieldwork is limited by the informants and the constraints of the fieldsite allows shifting perspectives and interpretations. That is, the nature of fieldwork and extrapolations from it should be viewed as narratives that grasp 'partial truths' (Abu Lughod 1990 Clifford 1986; Haraway 1988; Rosaldo 1989). Knowledge produced in the process of ethnographic inquiry is also situational and hence temporal/provisional (Cohen 1992).

With the above in mind, it was important for me to lay out my experiences of mobility, particularly with reference to Basel.

i. Getting to know Basel

I remember driving up the hill to our house in Munchenstein, fifteen minutes away from Basel City in the canton of Basel Land, on the day that we arrived in Switzerland. Our Swiss landlord was waiting to greet us and show us around our new home. It was very green and beautiful and quiet, in contrast to Dubai. Our Swiss adventure had started!

Over the first few days, we learnt about the special stickers for the rubbish bags, that rubbish collection took place on Tuesdays, that we would be fined if the bins were out on the wrong days, where to buy the bags — so much information and that was just about rubbish and recycling! We laughed! When I went to the supermarket for the first time with my husband, we spent hours making our purchase, most of the items were unrecognisable and we had to rely on Google Translate to find out what was what. We only purchased the basic staples that day. It took hours and the bill, when converted to UAE dirhams, was astonishing! 'Sticker shock,' we soon found out, was a common experience of foreigners when buying in Switzerland. School was due to start in a few days' time and our first priority was to organise everything at home.

Several standout incidents occurred over the course of the first few weeks and months:

1. I was looking for self-raising flour (a UK staple, which I soon learned was not available in this region) in Migros and, after combing the shelves, decided to ask a shop assistant. I started with the only German sentence that I knew: 'Sorry, do you speak English please?' She responded: '*Nein*' (no). Looking up the German words for 'flour' and 'pancakes', I proceed to pantomime flipping pancakes! This went on for a bit and the lady just gave me a hug, smiled and left!!

2. The first week in, I needed to see a hairdresser and used Google Maps to locate one near our house. I called the first number and asked in my only German sentence if he spoke English. The man just said *'Nein'* and put the phone down! I then looked up another number and called it using the same opening question. The lady hesitated and said *'Nein'* and then said 'no' in English. I immediately took advantage of the moment and told her in English that I was going to see her and proceeded to her salon and made an appointment using sign language and our phones (Google Translate) to communicate. Today she is one of my close Swiss friends. We started a language exchange coffee for her to learn English and for me to practise my German.
3. I started German language lessons a few months after our arrival. I began using whatever phrases I learnt straight away, even though I knew I was mangling the delivery. I was pleased to be learning and was trying to engage proactively and politely. I remember going into a coffee shop during the first week and ordering a coffee. The lady looked at me questioningly and I repeated myself. She looked at me blankly, so I apologised in German and said that I was learning. She responded 'Schlecht' in German, saying that it was bad! I remember feeling totally deflated by that remark.
4. A few weeks before Swiss National Day on August 1, we received an invitation in the letterbox from our neighbours to join the neighbourhood barbeque at their house. It was a lovely gesture and one that allowed us to meet everyone on our street. Our neighbours were cordial from the beginning and our relationship with them has only grown in warmth and friendliness, particularly after I invited them over for an Apero several months later.

Reminiscing now, I feel the emotion of each incident as I recount it. There have been countless interactions over the years in Basel that left an impression. Needless to say, when the children started school and I slowly began socialising and networking with others in the International School community, similarities in the experiences and stories exchanged was clear and it made me curious to explore further. 'Research is an extension of researchers' lives. Although most social scientists have been trained to guard against subjectivity (self-driven perspectives) and to separate self from research activities, it is an impossible task. Scholarship is inextricably connected to self—personal interest, experience, and familiarity' (Ngunjiri, Hernandez & Chang 2010: page reference).

ii. Learning By Doing

Like many newcomers to Basel, I spent a lot of time during the first few weeks here trawling information online, translating lots of documents, connecting with as many people as possible and spending time at school to help my family settle in. I signed up for German language classes and started looking for ways to spend my days meaningfully. From the outset, it was clear that there was a lot to get used to, particularly when it came to understanding how things worked here. There were so many rules! Upon reflection, it is clear that my background as a child who moved from country to country, and who was used to being in an environment where I did not understand the language (I moved to Kuwait from Scotland at the age of 9 and had to learn Arabic at school), or even the cultural norms, helped a lot. For several years during our time in Kuwait, we would go and visit extended family in Pakistan, where I was again exposed to another way of being; in short, I now realise that I am actually fine with not knowing the details of everyday interactions and not knowing a language very well. The resilience I built up over years of mobility and also displacement — during the Gulf War in 1990 — required me constantly to adapt to different environments. Looking back now, it is clear that this created a tremendous amount of flexibility in my attitude and outlook on life. Not everything in life is roses and that's ok.

In their 2014 article, 'Expatriate Adjustment: Considerations for Selection and Training', (http://dx.doi.org/10.1108/JGM-06-2013-0042), Feitosa, Kreutzer, Kramperth, Kramer, and Salas 'draw from a more theoretically driven conceptualization of adjustment, developed by Searle and Ward (1990), which suggests that adjustment is comprised of two distinct yet related facets: psychological and sociocultural. The psychological aspect refers to the emotional and mental well-being, and satisfaction of the expatriate, and the sociocultural dimension refers to the ability to 'fit in' and execute culturally appropriate behaviors (Searle and Ward1990). Upon arrival to the host country, expatriates are commonly faced with barriers to adjustment, such as the inability to speak the foreign language, coping with disorientation in the new environment, understanding the policies, customs, laws, and socializing with host country nationals (HCNs) (Black and Gregersen 1999; Tung 1981). One way to mitigate such obstacles of adjustment is to select on important traits and to provide appropriate training tools'. As noted above, those who are able to make the personal and professional adjustments are able to negotiate mobile transitions successfully.

It is this analysis that led to synthesising my research, coach training, participant observation and personal experiences. Learning-by-doing mobility led to the conceptualisation of *Sensorialscapes* as a process to experience and connect to a space. In my view, the flows of emotions carried by individuals are Capital that can be used to negotiate and create networks that stabilise and sustain. It is the intentionality of the process that, through my research, I have now been able to understand.

iii. University Experience

As the daughter of an academic, I have lived on several university campuses across the world and visited my father in his office on many occasions. It is a place where I feel at ease and one that 'embodies knowledge through sensory memory' (Sutton 2006) of connection and comfort. 'Skilled practice involves a mobilization of the mind/body within an environment, requiring constant and shifting use of judgement and dexterity within a changing environment' (Sutton 2006). It is this 'dexterity of judgement' that I feel has allowed me to explore and flourish despite many moments of uncertainty. The pull of university spaces and my curiosity to explore the possibility of pursuing a PhD in anthropology led me to Professor Picard's door at the University of Basel in 2015.

In chapter 7, on the Topography of Basel, I included the University of Basel as a space which encourages diversity and is in line with the imaginary of Basel City as an attractive destination. My first impression was received online, through the university website, when I was looking up teaching opportunities. Having been a Lecturer in Dubai, it made sense to start with that option; however, upon further investigation, it became clear that my unspoken wish to pursue a PhD was actually the best way forward. It was a frustrating experience trying to figure out the formalities. Each step took days of visiting various offices to find out more and, very quickly, I learned that the best way was to meet people face to face.

> 'There are plenty of support networks and organisations with lots of information online but there seems to be a gap between knowing where it is and how to access it. Being self-organised is important.'

Lorraine, participant in a Welcome Center workshop,University of Basel (2018)

The University of Basel is spread out across the city with a satellite made up of some really old buildings and also some modern, new structures, creating a different architectural aesthetic to that of Novartis and Roche (https://www.unibas.ch/en/Studies/My-Studies/Learning-Spaces.html). The spaces, for me, create a *Sensorialscape* of openness, gravitas and learning. It is where I started to build the network of peers who have supported me through this PhD process. It is where I have been challenged and, to be sure, there were many questions that I did not ask because I did not know what to ask! Within my department, as an Independent PhD candidate I felt supported and encouraged, but I had to rely on myself to push ahead through the unknown. At every stage, I had to investigate my options and decide on next steps. Looking back, I can see that I did a lot of unnecessary work, like learning and using software (MAXQDA) which added months to my workload without actually amounting to anything productive for me. In fact, I lost some interview data after transcribing it into the old version ... There were all sorts of delays and obstacles that complicated an already intense intellectual exercise. I often joked with my husband that it felt like I was doing two PhDs, having to understand how everything was done as well as delving deeper into my subject!

The location of our university department on the Rhine offered the opportunity to observe and explore the many sensorial practices and emotional expressions of everyday Basel life by the river: swimming and picnics in the summer, cycling, running and walking year round. The river is the heart of the city, providing plenty of opportunities to connect with and pass through it. As a conduit for physical mobility, providing transport links for the many barges, boats, sightseeing vessels, etc., coming from as far away as Amsterdam, the Rhine is an important part of the landscape.

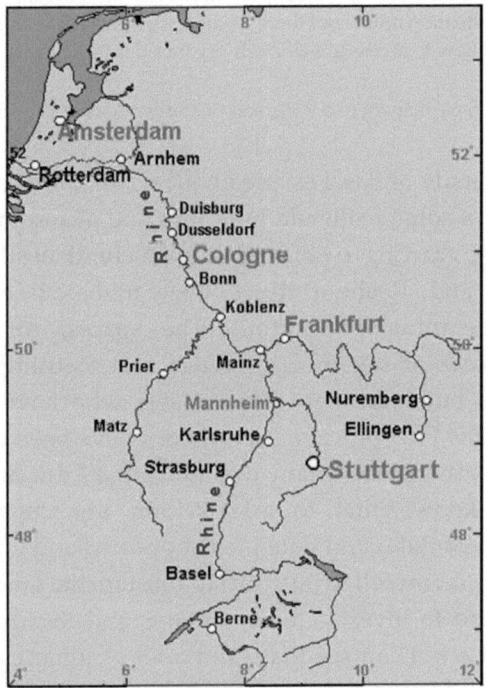

Figure 19. Map of the river Rhine, showing largest cities, islands and river names.
Source: Wikid77 (derivative of map from WP User:Geo_Swan, cropping & enlarging labels), CC BY-SA 3.0, via Wikimedia Commons

It is hard to have a conversation about Basel without mentioning the Rhine, such is its importance as part of the imaginary for both residents and travellers. As a researcher exploring mobility and the senses, it also became part of the interview process with people mentioning their walks/runs by the river, summer activities such as picnics and barbeques, and of course swimming in its waters.

> 'Have you tried Rhine swimming yet? It is a must do! Such a cool experience.'
>
> Chloe, spouse

iv. What does this mean?

In a sense, my love of anthropology has been an exploration of myself and my identity. Having visible identity markers — I have brown skin and dark hair — I am often asked where I am from, where I am really from. After I was born in London, my parents moved to Nigeria and then to Scotland, Kuwait, Oman, the United Arab Emirates, eventually retiring in Canada. I met my husband in Dubai, we moved to Hong Kong, then back to Dubai, and we are now in Basel. This nomadic existence has informed my ability to connect with people easily and it has also been an exercise in liminality: I look at ease but do not quite fit in. The space in between, the grey zone, ambiguity, belonging without quite being a part are all familiar feelings to which I have reconciled myself. 'The Third Culture Kid (TCK) builds relationships to all cultures, while not having full ownership in any' (Pollock & van Reken 2009).

Opportunities to live and travel have informed my personal perspectives and encouraged me to develop a global intercultural understanding. I have taken this further into researching the subject of mobility through an anthropological lens, in combination with personal development psychology. I have found that identity is a shifting construct in which one conveys who one is and how one has come to be that person. Some elements of the identity narrative are explored through challenges and experiences such as mobility, whilst other meaning is gained through framing internal and external dialogues. Agency in the narrative is achieved through the presentation of a self that can be used to connect to the present. It can be a coping mechanism or an intentional process. This is the construction of identity as I have experienced it, as I understand it, and also one that promotes personal development. It is this definition that I have used to inform my analysis, specifically because of the affluent amd mobile composition of my research group.

v. Conclusion

'Most people still think of themselves as belonging to a particular culture. Yet today, many of us who live in affluent societies choose aspects of our lives from a global "cultural supermarket", whether in terms of food, the arts or spiritual beliefs. So if roots are becoming simply one more consumer choice, can we still claim to possess a fundamental cultural identity?' (Mathews 2000).

The above excerpt is from the book *Global Culture/Individual Identity: Searching for Home in the Cultural Supermarket* by Professor Gordon Mathews, at the Chinese University of Hong Kong, where I did my Master's in anthropology. His book is about cultural identity and how it is often linked to a particular society which contains the codes and mores of a national culture. Access to the 'flows of globalisation' leads to the consumption of culture through the choices we make, such as food, clothes, music, etc. Gordon and I often engaged in discussions around the meaning of these choices and how they frame identity in this connected world.

The fluid nature of identity, what we choose to amplify and what we choose to minimise, depends on the significance we attach to seeking connection with or difference from others. Often the image we project on others is restrictive. At least that has been my personal experience when people have imposed an identity on me. The exploration of 'I' as a reflexive construct has led me to unpack the biases and assumptions we make when encountering difference. It provokes the imaginary of the self as creative, evolutionary and responsive to its environment.

Chapter 12 : Sensorialscapes

Memories, ideas, practices, materialities interact with Affect to create new forms of attachment, identification and placemaking for mobile individuals. The Emotional Capital that is built through 'continuous movement' operates as knowledge to shape time and space when locating oneself and forming a community. Through the chapters building up to this point, I have laid out the various aspects of my research, giving glimpses into the lives of Corporate Executives and their families in Basel. The complexity of my field led me to curb my curiosity in order to present an overall picture, one which can be used to delve deeper into areas of particular interest.

In this chapter, I seek to synthesise the multiple perspectives brought up previously through the analytical lens of *Sensorialscapes*.

i. Linking Spatialities

Global interconnectedness — the movement of people, goods, ideas, objects and capital — allows the actors involved to engage in complex performance activities. Mobile families make meaning through practices that evoke memories of past relationships and places, and this meaning-making involves a concurrent transmission of emotions that connect with the present. The process is fluid and forms a part of mobility; it does not come before or after. The senses play a key role in providing the knowledge necessary to connect through a 'product/object' such as food, a custom, music, smells, personal artefacts, etc., thus allowing the (conscious) manipulation of emotions to create a feeling of belonging.

I met with a Corporate spouse who moved to Basel 6 months earlier. She explained that she was familiar with 'the feeling of being new and starting again and how [I] had to find [my] particular foods, a good doctor, meet people and ground [myself] with the idea that time will make it easier to settle in'. Feelings are an integral part of social activity and interaction with people and spaces. Recognising that the process of mobility requires time and connection empowers actors to negotiate the uncertainty that invariably arises. The migratory experience often relies on sensorial input through embodied emotions and the memories associated with them. Objects have a particular meaning ascribed to them and this value is constructed socially through rituals or performances such as Thanksgiving or Christmas. Emotions are carried and shared by individuals as discourse, practice, relationships and imaginaries. They offer a pattern of sensory meanings through which to perceive and embody experiences, communicating inwards and outwards.

ii. Emotional Capital

The different types of Capital that can be acquired by individuals as a way to further their career trajectory point to accumulation over time and across space. The diversity of experiences adds a level of understanding which increases Emotional Intelligence and therefore enhances the ability to deal with ambiguity and uncertainty. This also plays into the personal sphere where mobility enables individuals to stretch their experiences and step out of their comfort zone. I argue that the insights gained through this lifestyle broaden and develop individuals at an emotional level.

When I attended a workshop entitled 'Family Survival Skills for International Living' at the ISB last year, the topic of TCKs came up. In their book *Third Culture Kids: Growing Up Among Worlds*, Pollock and van Reken capture the essence of 'stories about all places' as a way to showcase the innate sense of growing up 'highly mobile and genuinely cross-cultural'. I bring this up only to extrapolate the connection between mobility and high levels of adaptability by pushing the boundaries of identity construction. 'Ultimately it is the sense of being understood in our experience that is the most healing' (Frankl 1946).

If we view memory and the senses as active, creative and transformational cultural processes (Korsmeyer & Sutton 2015), then it follows that some of these categories shape our perceptions of the world. There are various types of memories (personal, collective, semantic, event, bodily) that feed into the aspirational narrative of cosmopolitanism and the 'mobile imaginary', and these in turn build different kinds of Capital that facilitate the navigation of unfamiliar lived complexity. Being exposed to new ways of being can provoke anxiety within individuals, which is why Emotional Intelligence is a keenly sought-after skill. Peter Salovey and Jack Mayer, who created the term 'emotional intelligence' (as used today), describe it as 'the ability to perceive emotions, to access and generate emotions so as to assist thought, to understand emotions and emotional meanings, and to reflectively regulate emotions in ways that promote emotional and intellectual growth' (Stein & Book 2011).

iii. Discomfort Explored

Feelings of strangeness trigger many different emotions that can unsettle individuals. Perception and memory connect the body to material culture, which is why comfort food, personal objects, etc., help reinforce positive and familiar feelings. If we consider food, the emotional bond is not only between the individual and food but also between the individual and others and the memories the food evokes; it nourishes the soul as well as the body (Locher et al 2005). Comfort foods create belonging, safety, connection to spaces and people. Food often reflects mobility and temporality, providing clues into personal journeys.

Discomfort, on the other hand, leads to disconnection and feelings of strangeness, a lack of order, a break from habit and loss of familiarity. Eating unfamiliar food for the first time can be stressful, distasteful and even disgusting. These are some of the emotions that arise and it is only after several tries that some foods can be enjoyed. Cultural exploration through food is one way to experience new destinations when travelling. It is curious to note how certain once 'exotic' foods such as sushi or couscous have now become mainstream. In fact, sampling different types of cuisines is considered cosmopolitan and trendy; it can bestow status and power through Cultural Capital.

'Familiar food can play an important role in the migratory context; both at a public visible level and also, and overall, in the intimate domain of the domestic sphere and the mundane everyday. As migration involves discontinuity with the known human, cultural and material environment, food practices and preferences can be used as a strategy to, in a sensorial way, fight off the sense of fragmentation triggered by migration' (Mata-Codesal 2008).

iv. Conclusion

The social nature of food as an object of interaction with people and places, as well as the meaning it has, is often used to negotiate difficult experiences, such as transitions, by cooking comfort food. The narrative around food is not exact because of the nature of the senorial experience and how it is constructed. What is clear is the visceral nature of the connection it can evoke over time and space. Being able to leverage and negotiate *Sensorialscapes*, by understanding what a mobile individual requires when settling into a new environment, is a skill that can be learned. Food is an example of a strategy often used by newcomers to negotiate new spaces and claim their place through cooking and eating familiar foods, thus connecting to the past, creating the present and also imagining the future. As a multisensorial object, food has an innate power to connect on multiple levels.

Chapter 13. Concluding Findings and Remarks

'One of the analytical advantages of mobility studies, a relatively novel field of study, is that it shows us how imagination (a dynamic psychological process) and imaginaries (products of the imagination) are crucial for very different forms of human (im)mobility' (Salazar 2020: page reference).

In this dissertation, I have set out to explore the experiences of Corporate Executives and their families with a particular focus on the Pharmaceutical Industry in Basel. I have presented my research based on narrative interviews, participant observation and used theoretical frameworks to explore the individual journey as part of global mobility. By connecting the local to the global through the individual I summarise my findings below and add my final concluding remarks.

1. Mobility enhances career and personal trajectories

This is not a new finding; however, it does underline the reason why Mobility is much sought after by companies and employees alike. Sharing the biographical experience of my informants, it is clear that whilst many different motivations may have been expressed, international assignments are directly connected to career advancement. The perceived difficulties and disruptions that may arise as a result of mobility are trumped by this single motivator. When exploring the impact on families, spouses often cited new opportunities for their children and, secondarily, for themselves.

Approaching mobility through a multidisciplinary set of lenses set within an anthropological framework, I used literature from psychology, cultural studies, HR, identity & belonging, sensorial flows, and globalisation to analyse and synthesise transnational and migration processes. The shaping of Mobile trajectories through this intersection of disciplines has allowed me to open up further areas of exploration whilst acknowledging individual journeys as unique and reflective of this life.

2. Intellectual Capital leads to Mobility and Mobility leads to Intellectual Capital

The Corporate Executives whom I interviewed were all senior managers leading large business portfolios. Their skills as experts in a given area was determined and tested through their performance. Mobility was acknowledged as a factor contributing to their success as Business Leaders. It gave them the additional Leadership skills necessary to deal with ambiguity and uncertainty with agility. The Personal Development created by mobility is understood to add to the business environment through the acknowledgement of diversity. Living in various locations leads to making business and personal adjustments and to the accrual of inclusive practices.

This circulation of Skills, Knowledge and Capital accrual through mobility is one of the main drivers for companies when it comes to their Talent Management programmes. Once an individual is identified as a High Potential Performer, a path across several geographies is laid out. Questions around the efficacy and cost of this approach are being raised more and more by multiple stakeholders; however, till there a more attentive and individualised programme which tracks leadership and personal development is found, the process cannot be justifiably determined. All parties will engage to further their own objectives.

3. Emotional Capital Accumulation

Building on Intellectual Capital, I found that handling the many emotions (Emotional Capital) that arose through mobility required a good degree of Emotional Intelligence. This finding leaned on the literature highlighting the importance of an individual's mindset in overcoming and accommodating challenges through resilience and agility. Curiosity and flexibility allow for an open personal orientation, one which does not block difference through fear. The ability to rely on oneself to meaningfully connect to a space through awareness of the senses (*Sensorialscapes*), to fully engage with the surroundings to create networks, requires receptivity and an understanding of how to negotiate the emotional cues on offer.

The resulting accrual of Emotional Capital can be discerned in the narratives employed by individuals to discuss their choices, their relationships, their world views; it allows for less rigidity in relation to self and others. Some critics find that it loosens the hold of nationalism, but this has remained unaddressed as it lies beyond the scope of this study.

4. Agency

There is no 'one size fits all' solution regarding the approach to mobility and, whilst the informants in my field may be constrained at certain points both in their career and life choices, they had a good degree of Agency, which I found proportional to their experience. Having accrued several forms of Capital, they were in a position to negotiate more benefits for themselves and their families. Exceptions and allowances (such as contract renewals, permit extensions, tax benefits, etc.) are used to retain, accommodate and reward performance. Career choices are therefore not necessarily impacted by documentation or official requirements, but by relationships and networks.

The constraints to Agency are defined by structural (e.g. government regulations, company policies, etc.) and individual (career trajectory, family life cycle, aspiration, etc.) factors. The combination of the two can either facilitate or hinder mobility when certain 'boxes' need to be ticked in order to take the next step.

5. Culture & Belonging

Culture as practised in everyday interactions through *Sensorialscapes* focuses on connecting to a space through the five senses and memory, embodying experiential relationships between self, others and the environment.

Company culture can be created by focusing on the meaning behind actions that promote productive and effective professional relationships: building a sense of belonging to leverage trust and best practices through a clear understanding of expectations and obligations, focusing on the how and the why, and adopting mechanisms that feed back into the organisation at every level. The support on offer through learning and personal development is clear; however, the inability to close the loop through solutions to understanding the barriers that arise in practice means that gaps occur. Belonging at the individual level requires a level of empathy and non-judgemental acceptance from both sides. Representation and the ability to engage are critical factors in creating networks that support inclusion.

Sensorialscapes often rely on materiality as a way to connect. Objects become carriers of emotions and, whilst this may be recognised, the thrust of my research was to highlight the importance and criticality of this in order to leverage the ability to connect and create networks that support change. This links to the well-being of the individual negotiating both familiarity and discomfort in the complex relationship between mobility and success. A holistic approach attuned to this concept via a Sponsor (particularly in a company) can mitigate the various adjustment gaps that arise.

6. Loose Ends

Spouses, often the 'invisible employees' who need to 'learn by doing', are exposed to the realities of new environments abruptly and uncomfortably. Their experiences can sometimes be downplayed and undervalued, but their stake in the support and adjustment of their families is instrumental to success. This has been confirmed in the HR literature. However, a gap that I found in Basel was that the wealth of skills, knowledge and experience of this group remained an untapped resource. The insights and Capital garnered by spouses can provide support and, in many cases, also actually lead to viable employment if only the recruitment process were more accepting, diverse and inclusive. Whilst the support offered included networking opportunities and career advice to some spouses, it is clear that more needs to be done to actively engage with the often highly skilled other half, particularly if they are looking to become gainfully employed.

Changing and shaping the conversation around recruitment processes would make companies more attractive, providing an additional value-add to a culture that values belonging through a broader commitment to families.

i. Complexity of Success

'Thinking is not on the Move, People are'

Prof. Walter Leimgruber

This remark was made at a workshop focusing on the Mobility of the Highly Skilled to Switzerland. It expresses the opposite of 'Globally Mobile Intellectual Capital', the title of my thesis, in which I have looked at flows and the accumulation of Capital which inform Thinking, that is, if we view the interplay of Emotions and Skills broadly. Where the success factors of mobility within this context are concerned, it is clear that:

- Individuals need certain skills to fulfil specific roles that in turn facilitate positive outcomes during international assignments.
- Often the areas central to an organisation's success place more value on mobility, e.g. research fosters collaboration through global expertise.
- Individuals tend to get ahead with the support of career development assistance and familial attention.
- Categorisation fails to perceive the value of relationships, processes and opportunities to leverage diversity.
- Performance and Adjustment are related. Individual capabilities become visible due to mobility.
- Policies shape the environment for mobility; participation is often unequal due to decisions and conditions within companies/countries.

A multilevel approach acknowledging the complex nature of job mobility allows the implementation of supportive measures to facilitate success. Recognising the structural and individual factors at play, as they arise, ensures a greater degree of flexibility and transparency. A better understanding of mobility leverages the diffusion of knowledge, innovation, technology, etc., and thus stimulates the Intellectual Capital of an organisation. 'It is hardly possible to separate these different levels of mobility and they are important when looking at biographical narrations and the wider picture of how people create their lives and careers' (Sontag 2018: page reference).

ii. Mobility & Identity Markers

A unified approach to mobility, which would examine the general category of movement in its full range, is problematic because all forms and types of mobility are deeply imbued with cultural meanings and should be studied within the specific cultural, economic and social conditions in which they are created (Glick Schiller & Salazar 2013). 'Food has long been understood as a potent marker of cultural identity. In the context of transnational migrant communities, food practices express group and individual identities as well as multiple social positionings within the current environment. At the same time, food practices are part of navigating between local and global attachments' (Beagan & Chapman 2013). Exploring the senses through food opens the discourse to Affect, Emotions and Connection. This framework can be further explored to conceptualise the meaning behind other identity markers (such as gender, ethnicity and race) through the lens of mobility. The categories within which people position themselves as well as how they are positioned structurally create a new set of questions to analyse.

iii. Globalisation, Self & Ethnography

According to the anthropologist Laura Nader (https://anthropology.berkeley.edu/laura-nader), anthropology's strength is its reflexivity. Our humanistic perspective allows ethnography to be at once scientific and reflexive. Modern ethnographers must think about how their own positions and ideas affect their conclusions. For me to start by looking at the interaction between Globalisation processes and the Self was challenging. It brought up the dichotomy between myself as a researcher in the field, with my own experiences of mobility, and the societal processes and relations involved in corporate mobility vis-à-vis my professional perspective as a Coach and Trainer. This complex set of perspectives required me to constantly question relationships, assumptions and the often 'neat' conclusions produced by a certain logic. Challenging social and personal constructions throughout this thesis has led to a multidisciplinary approach incorporating and threading together my areas of interest and expertise. I set out to understand the implications of mobility on Corporate Executives and their families in a nuanced and methodical manner so as to understand how to create Belonging in a Mobile world.

iv. PhD 2015 – Pandemic 2020

As I finish writing this thesis, Covid 19 has wrought a new world of social distancing, working from home, lockdown rules and quarantine protocols, to name just a few of the major changes. This pandemic, with the closing of borders, has certainly challenged the movement that many take for granted. The implications on work culture have yet to be fully realised, but conversations on how to deal with half the workforce engaging remotely are currently underway. How this will affect Corporate Mobility is still unknown, but the few conversations I have had point towards a new way of building work relations.

In the five years since the start of this project both Novartis and Roche have gone through several change initiatives. In 2018, Novartis welcomed a new CEO, Vas Narasimhan, who had a new vision to Reimagine Medicine. The company has been moulding its culture to align with this mission. Roche has also undergone a cultural transformation by adopting an Agile approach. Both companies are constantly in the process of reviewing their organisations to ensure agility and purpose. Building relationships and connections to support work objectives are key drivers for success.

References

Abdul Malek, M. (2014). Sources of support and expatriation: A multiple stakeholder perspective of expatriate adjustment and performance in Malaysia. *International journal of human resource management*, 26(2), pp. 258-276. doi:10.1080/09585192.2014.937968

Abu-Lughod, Lila, and Lutz, Catherine. (1990). Introduction: Emotion, Discourse, and the Politics of Everyday Life. In C. Lutz and L. Abu-Lughod (eds.). *Language and the Politics of Emotion*. 1-23. Cambridge: Cambridge University Press

Ackers, Louise (2005). Moving People and Knowledge: Scientific Mobility in the European Union. *International Migration*, 43:99-131

Ahmed, S. (2004a). Affective Economies. *Social Text*, 22: 117-139

Ahmed, S. (2004b). *Cultural Politics of Emotion*. Routledge

Amanda Wise & Selvaraj Velayutham (2017). Transnational Affect and Emotion in Migration Research, *International Journal of Sociology*, 47:2, 116-130, DOI: 10.1080/00207659.2017.1300468

Anderson E. N. (2005) Food Classification and Communication, *Everyone Eats*, New York University Press

Andreason, W.A. (2008). Expatriate Adjustment of Spouses and Expatriate Managers: An Integrative Research Review. *International Journal of Management*.

Appadurai, A. (1995) .The production of locality, in: R. Fardon (Ed.) *Counterworks: Managing the Diversity of Knowledge*. 204-225, Routledge

Appadurai, A. (1996). *Modernity at Large: Cultural Dimensions of Globalisation*, University of Minnesota Press

Appadurai, A. (1999), Globalization and the research imagination. *International Social Science Journal*, 51: 229-238. https://doi:10.1111/1468-2451.00191

Baldassar, L. (2007). *Transnational Families and the Provision of Moral and Emotional Support: The Relationship Between Truth and Distance*. Identities Yverdon, Switzerland. 14(4), 385-409. doi:10.1080/10702890701578423

Bastia, T. (2014). Intersectionality, migration and development. Progress in *Development Studies*, 14(3), 237-248. https://doi.org/10.1177/1464993414521330

Beagan, B., & Chapman, G. (2013). Food Practices and Transnational Identities: Case Studies of Two Punjabi-Canadian Families. Food, Culture and Society: An International Journal of Multidisciplinary Research.

Beaverstock, J. V. (2002). Transnational elites in global cities: British expatriates in Singapore's financial district. *Geoforum*, 33(4), pp. 525-538. doi:10.1016/s0016-7185(02)00036-2

Beck, U. (2000). The cosmopolitan perspective: Sociology of the second age of modernity. *The British journal of sociology*, 51(1), pp. 79-105. doi:10.1080/000713100358444

Benson, M. (2009). Migration and the Search for a Better Way of Life: A Critical Exploration of Lifestyle Migration. *The Sociological Review*, 57(4), pp. 608-625. doi:10.1111/j.1467-954X.2009.01864.x

Boccagni, P. (2015). Emotions on the move: Mapping the emergent field of emotion and migration. *Emotion, space and society*, 16, pp. 73-80. doi:10.1016/j.emospa.2015.06.009

Bolino, M. C. (2007). Expatriate assignments and intra-organizational career success: Implications for individuals and organizations. *Journal of International Business Studies*, 38(5), pp. 819-835. doi:10.1057/palgrave.jibs.8400290

Bourdieu, P. (1986). The forms of capital. In J. Richardson (Ed.) Handbook of Theory and Research for the Sociology of Education. New York, Greenwood, 241-258

Bourdieu, Pierre (1990). *The Logic of Practice*. Polity Press

Briggs, J. (1970), *Never in Anger: Portrait of an Eskimo Family*. Harvard University Press

Burrell, K. (2012). The Objects of Christmas: The Politics of Festive Materiality in the Lives of Polish Immigrants. In M. Svasek (ed.), *Moving Subjects, Moving Objects: Migrant Art, Artefacts and Emotional Agency*. Berghahn

Bull M., Mitchell J. P (2015) *Ritual, performance and the senses*.

Camenisch, A., & Mueller, S. (2017). From (E)Migration to Mobile Lifestyles: Ethnographic and Conceptual Reflections about Mobilities and Migration. *New Diversities Journal*, 19(3), 43–57

Certeau, M. d. (2002). *The practice of everyday life* ([2nd. ed.].). University of California Press

Chamberlain, M. & Leydesdorff, S. (2004). Transnational families: Memories and narratives, *Global Networks*, 4(3), pp. 227–241

Chin, E. (2016). *Migration, media and global-local spaces*. Palgrave Macmillan

Choo S. (2004). Eating Satay Babi: sensory perception of transnational movement, *Journal of Intercultural Studies*, 25:3, 203-213

Chun Guo & Akram Al Ariss (2015). Human resource management of international migrants: current theories and future research, *The International Journal of Human Resource Management*, 26:10, 1287-1297, DOI: 10.1080/09585192.2015.1011844

Classen, C. (1997). Foundations for an anthropology of the senses. *International Social Science Journal*, 49: 401-412. doi:10.1111/j.1468-2451.1997.tb00032.x

Clifford, J and G.E. Marcus. (1986). *Writing Culture: The Poetics and Politics of Ethnography*. University of California Press

Cohen, J. (1992). A power primer. *Psychological Bulletin*, 112(1), 155–159. https://doi.org/10.1037/0033-2909.112.1.155

Coles, A. and Fechter, A.M. (2008). Gender and Family among Transnational Professionals. New York: Routledge (Introduction)

Conradson, D & Mckay, D. (2007). Translocal Subjectivities: Mobility, Connection, Emotion, *Mobilities*, 2:2, 167-174, DOI: 10.1080/17450100701381524

Cottingham, M. D. (2016). Theorizing emotional capital. *Theory and society*, 45(5), pp. 451-470. https://doi:10.1007/s11186-016-9278-7

Davidson, J. (2004). Spatialising affect; affecting space: An introduction. *Gender, Place & Culture*, 11(3), pp. 373-374. doi:10.1080/0966369042000258686

Davoine, Eric, and Ravasi Claudio (2013). The Challenge of Dual Career Expatriate Management in a Specific Host National Environment: An Exploratory Study of Expatriate and Spouse Adjustment in Switzerland Based MNCs. *Fses Working Papers*: n. pag. Print

Douglas, M. T. (2010). Standard Social Uses of Food.. In *Food in the Social Order: Studies of Food and Festivities in Three American Communities*, Edited by: Douglas, M. D. New York: Russell Sage Foundation. E. Farndale et al./Journal of World Business 45 1984a. 161 – 168

Duchêne-Lacroix, C., M. Götzö, and K. Sontag. (2016). The Experience of Multilocal Living: Mobile Immobilities or Immobile Mobilities? In M. Gutekunst, A. Hackl, S. Leoncini, J. S. Schwarz, I. Götz (eds.), *Bounded Mobilities. Ethnographic Perspectives on Social Hierarchiesand Global Inequalities*, (pp.265-282), transcript Verlag

Duruz, J. (2011). Tastes of hybrid belonging: Following the laksa trail in Katong, Singapore. *Continuum*, 25(5), pp. 605-618. doi:10.1080/1030 4312.2011.597843

Erdal, M. B. and Oeppen, C. (2013) Migrant Balancing Acts: Understanding the Interactions Between Integration and Transnationalism, *Journal of Ethnic and Migration Studies*, 39(6), pp. 867–884

Faist, T., Fauser, M., & Kivisto, P. (2011). *The migration-development nexus: A transnational perspective*. Palgrave Macmillan

Farndale, E., Scullion, H., & Sparrow, P. (2010). The role of the corporate HR function in global talent management. *Journal of World Business*, 45, 161-168

Feitosa, J., Kreutzer, C., Kramperth, A., Kramer, W.S., Salas, E. (2014). Expatriate Adjustment: Considerations for Selection and Training, *Journal of Global Mobility*, Vol 2 Iss 2 pp. 134 – 159

Feld, Steven. (2005). Places Sensed, Senses Placed: Toward a Sensuous Epistemology of Environments. In *Empire of the Senses: The Sensual Culture Reader*, 179-191

Frankl, V. (1946). *Man's Search for Meaning*. ISBN 9780807014295

Gayatri Gopinath. (2010). "Archive, Affect, and the Everyday: Queer Diasporic Re-Visions" in J. Staiger, A. Cvetkovich, A, Reynolds (eds.). *Political Emotions*. Routledge

Geertz, C. (1971), After the Revolution: The Fate of Nationalism in the New States, in: Geertz, C. (1973), *The Interpretation of Cultures*. Basic Books, 234-254

Geertz, C. (1972). Religious Change and Social Order in Soeharto's Indonesia. *Asia*, 27, 62-84.

Geertz, Clifford (1973). "Thick Description: Toward an Interpretive Theory of Culture", *The Interpretation of Cultures: Selected Essays*, New York: Basic Books, pp. 3–30

Gisbert, Pascual. Social Facts in Durkheim's System. *Anthropos*, vol. 54, no. 3/4, 1959, pp. 353-369. JSTOR, www.jstor.org/stable/40454241. Accessed 2 May 2020

Glick Schiller, N., Basch, L. and Blanc Szanton, C. (1992) Towards a transnationalization of migration: Race, class, ethnicity and nationalism reconsidered. *The Annals of the New York Academy of Sciences*, 645, 1-24

Glick Schiller, N. (2013). Regimes of Mobility Across the Globe. *Journal of ethnic and migration studies*, 39(2), pp. 183-200. doi:10.1080/1369183x.2013.723253

Hannerz, U. (1990). 'Cosmopolitans and Locals in World Culture', in Mike Featherstone (ed), *Global Culture: Nationalism, Globalization and Modernity*. London: Sage

Hannerz, U. (1996). *Transnational Connections: Culture, People, Places*. Routledge

Hannerz, U. (2016). Cosmopolitans and Locals in World Culture. *Theory, culture & society*, 7(2-3), pp. 237-251. doi:10.1177/026327690007002014

Hannerz, U. (2009). Transnational connections (Transferred to digital printing.). Routledge

Haraway, D. (1988). Situated Knowledges: The Science Question in Feminism and the Privilege of Partial Perspective. *Feminist Studies*, 14 (3), 575-599. https://doi.org/10.2307/3178066

Harvard Business Review: Strategic Global Mobility (2014).

Herod, Andrew. (1999). Reflections on interviewing foreign elites: Praxis, positionality, validity, and the cult of the insider. *Geoforum*, 30.4: 313--327

Howes, D. (1996). The Senses Still: Perception and Memory as Material Culture in Modernity. C. Nadia Seremetakis, ed. *American Anthropologist*, 98(1), pp. 201-202. doi:10.1525/aa.1996.98.1.02a 00500

Howes D. (2003). Coming to Our Senses. The Sensual Turn in Anthropological Understanding, in: *Sensual Relations: Engaging the Senses in Culture and Social Theory*, Michigan: University of Michigan Press, pp. 29-58

Howes, D, M L Schwimmer, J Rousseau, S van Wyck, and C Trott. (1987). Olfaction and transition: An essay on the ritual uses of smell. *Canadian Review of Sociology and Anthropology*. 24 (3): 398-416

Howes D. (ed). (2014) A cultural history of the senses in the Modern Age.

Jacobs-Huey, L. (2002), The Natives Are Gazing and Talking Back: Reviewing the Problematics of Positionality, Voice, and Accountability among "Native" Anthropologists. *American Anthropologist*, 104: 791–804. doi:10.1525/aa.2002.104.3.791

Julie L. Locher PhD, William C. Yoels, Donna Maurer & Jillian van Ells. (2005). Comfort Foods: An Exploratory Journey Into The Social and Emotional Significance of Food, *Food and Foodways*, 13:4, 273-297, DOI: 10.1080/07409710500334509

Kaufmann, V. (2004). Motility: Mobility as capital. *International journal of urban and regional research*, 28(4), pp. 745-756. doi:10.1111/j.0309-1317.2004.00549.x

Korsmeyer, C. Sutton, D. (2011). The Sensory Experience of Food. *Food, Culture & Society*, 14(4), pp. 461-475. doi:10.2752/175174411X13046 092851316

KPMG (2013): International Assignment Policies and Practices of Swiss Headquartered Companies.

Kunz, S. (2016). Privileged Mobilities: Locating the Expatriate in Migration Scholarship. *Geography compass*, 10(3), pp. 89-101. doi:10.1111/gec3.12253

Larsen, J. (2006). Geographies of Social Networks: Meetings, Travel and Communications. *Mobilities*, 1(2), pp. 261-283. doi:10.1080/17450 100600726654

Law L. (2001). Home Cooking: Filipino Women and Geographies of the Senses in Hong Kong, *Ecumene*, vol. 8, no. 3

Levitt, P. and Nina Glick Schiller (2004). Conceptualizing Simultaneity: A Transnational Social Field Perspective on Society. *The International Migration Review*. 38 (3), 1002-1039

Locher J.L., Yoels W. C.,Maurer D. & van Ells J. (2005). Comfort Foods: An Exploratory Journey Into The Social and Emotional Significance of Food, *Food and Foodways*, 13:4, 273-297

Lutz, Catherine, and Geoffrey White. (1986). The Anthropology of Emotions. *Annual Review of Anthropology*, 15 : 405-36

Mahadevan, Jasmin (2009). Redefining Organizational Cultures: An Interpretative Anthropological Approach to Corporate Narratives [72 paragraphs]. *Forum Qualitative Sozialforschung / Forum: Qualitative Social Research*, 10(1), Art. 44, http://nbn-resolving.de/urn:nbn: de:0114-fqs0901440

Maréchal, Garance. (2010). Autoethnography. In A. J. Mills, G. Durepos & E. Wiebe (Eds.), *Encyclopedia of case study research* (Vol. 2, pp. 43-45). Thousand Oaks, CA: Sage Publications

Massumi, B. (2015). *The Politics of Affect*. Polity Press

Mata-Codesal, D. (2008). Rice & Coriander. Sensorial re-creations of home through food. *Ecuadorians in a Northern Spanish City. Working paper*, University of Sussex

Mathews, G. (2000). *Global Culture/Individual Identity: Searching for Home in the Cultural Supermarket*. Routledge

McKay D. (2005). Migration and the Sensuous Geographies of Re-emplacement in the Philippines. *Journal of Intercultural Studies*, Vol. 26, Nos. 1 /2, February /May 2005, pp. 75-91

Meier L. (ed.) (2015) Migrant professionals in the city: local encounters, identities and inequalities.

Milton K., Svasek, M., (2005). *Mixed Emotions: Anthropological Studies of Feeling*. Oxford: Berghahn, 1 23.

Miriam Moeller, Jane Maley, Michael Harevy & Timothy Kiessling (2015): Global Talent Management and Inpatriate Social Capital Building: A Status Inconsistency Perspective, *The International Journal of Human Resource Management*, DOI: 10.1080/09585192.2015.1052086.

Morokvasic, M. (2004). 'Settled in mobility': Engendering post-wall migration in Europe. *Feminist review*, 77(1), pp. 7-25. doi:10.1057/palgrave.fr.9400154

Nelson, L. W. (1996) Hands in the Chit'lins: Notes on Native Anthropological Re- search among African American Women. In G. Etter-Lewis and M. Foster (eds.), *Unrelated Kin: Race and Gender in Women's Personal Narratives*. 183-199. Routledge

Ng, T. W. H. (2007). Determinants of job mobility: A theoretical integration and extension. *Journal of occupational and organizational psychology*, 80(3), pp. 363-386. doi:10.1348/096317906x130582

Ngunjiri, F. W., Hernandez, K. C., & Chang, H. (2010). Living autoethnography: Connecting life and research [Editorial].*Journal of Research Practice*,6 (1), Article E1. Retrieved [date of access], from http://jrp.icaap.org/index.php/jrp/article/view/241/186

Nunes-Reichel, J. and M. Santiago-Delefosse. (2015). The Experience of Skilled Migrant Women in Switzerland: Challenges for Social and Professional Integration. *International Journal of Humanities and Social Science*. vol. 5, no. 4(1), April 2015. https://www.academia.edu/12484203/The_Experience_of_Skilled_Migrant_Women_in_Sw itzerland_Challenges_for_Social_and_Professional_Integration

Panteleou, M. (2017). Mobile people- mobile ethnographer: Thinking about cultural mobilities. 5th International Conference *The Migration Conference*, 23 - 26 August 2017, Harokopio University, Athens

Picard, Jacques., Chakkalakal, S. and Andris, S. (eds.) (2016) *Grenzen aus kultur-wissenschaftlichen Perspektiven*. Panama Verlag. Available at: https://www.panama-verlag.de/programm/grenzen/

Pollock, D. C., & Van Reken, R. E. (2009). *Third culture kids* (Revised edition.). Brealey

Pool, S.W. (2000). Organizational Culture and Its Relationship between Job Tension in Measuring Outcomes among Business Executives. *Journal of Management Development*, 19, 32-49.

Purgał-Popiela, Joanna. (2011). Adjustment of Expatriates and Their Spouses as a Challenge for International Human Resource Management. *Journal of Intercultural Management*, Vol. 3, No. 1, pp. 27–43.

Purgał-Popiela, J. (2016). Developing Cross-cultural Competences through International Employees Flow – Experience of Subsidiaries Providing Business Services. *Journal of Intercultural Management*, 8(3), pp. 87-103

Rössel, J. (2015). *Cosmopolitan cultural consumption: Preferences and practices in a heterogenous, urban population in Switzerland*. Poetics (Amsterdam), 50, pp. 80-95. doi:10.1016/j.poetic.2015.02.009

Rabinow, P. (1977). *Reflections on Fieldwork in Morocco*. University of California Press

Resler, R, F. Incocciati, and A. Quarck. (2018). *The Trailing Spouse Reimagined, Stories of People Transported by Love.* Bergli Books

Rojek, C., & Urry, J. (1997). Touring cultures. Routledge

Rosaldo, R. (1989). *Culture and Truth: The Remaking of Social Analysis.* Beain Press

Ryan, L. (2008). "Navigating the Emotional Terrain of Families "Here" and "There": Women, Migration and the Management of Emotions." *Journal of intercultural studies*, 29(3), pp. 299-313. doi:10.1080/07256860802169238

Salazar, N. B. (2011). Anthropological Takes on (Im)Mobility. *Identities*, 18(6), pp. i-ix. doi:10.1080/1070289X.2012.683674

Salazar, N. B. (2008). The Anxieties of Mobility: Migration and Tourism in the Indonesian Borderlands. Crossroads: *An Interdisciplinary Journal of Southeast Asian Studies*, 19(2), pp. 172-174

Salazar, N.B. (2010). *Envisioning Eden: Mobilizing imaginaries in tourism and beyond.* Oxford: Berghahn Books

Salazar, N. B., & Salazar, N. B. (2015). Becoming Cosmopolitan through Traveling? Some Anthropological Reflections. *The Journal of English Language and Literature*, 61(1), 51–67. https://doi.org/10.15794/JELL.2015.61.1.004

Salazar, N. B. (2020). On imagination and imaginaries, mobility and immobility: Seeing the forest for the trees. *Culture & Psychology*. https://doi.org/10.1177/1354067X20936927

Sandoz, L. (2019). *Mobilities of the Highly Skilled towards Switzerland. The Role of Intermediaries in Defining "Wanted Immigrants".* Springer Open

Schein, E. (1992). *Organizational Culture and Leadership: A Dynamic View.* Jossey-Bass

Schema Kulturelle Topographien (2011). "Zentrum für Kulturelle Topografien" of the University of Basel. https://kultop.philhist.unibas.ch/de/home/

Schiller, N. G. (1992). Transnationalism: A New Analytic Framework for Understanding Migration: A New Analytic Framework. Annals of the New York Academy of Sciences, 645(1 Towards a Tra), pp. 1-24. doi:10.1111/j.1749-6632.1992.tb33484.x

Schrooten, M. (2016). Living in mobility: Trajectories of Brazilians in Belgium and the UK. *Journal of Ethnic and Migration Studies*, 42(7), pp. 1199-1215. doi:10.1080/1369183X.2015.1089160.

Seremetakis, N. C., (1994). *The Senses Still: Perception and Memory as Material Culture in Modernity.* Routledge

Skrbiš, Z. (2008). Transnational Families: Theorising Migration, Emotions and Belonging. *Journal of intercultural studies*, 29(3), pp. 231-246. doi:10.1080/07256860802169188

Sontag, K. (2018). *Mobile entrepreneurs*. Budrich UniPress

Srinivas, T. (2006). 'As Mother Made It': The Cosmopolitan Indian Family,'Authentic' Food and the Construction of Cultural Utopia. *International Journal of Sociology of the Family*.

Stein, S. J., & Book, H. E. (2011). *The EQ edge: Emotional intelligence and your success*. Jossey-Bass

Sutton, J. (2006). Introduction: Memory, Embodied Cognition, and the Extended Mind. *Philosophical Psychology*, 19(3), 281–289. doi: 10.1080/09515080600702550

Sutton, D. (2010). Food and the Senses. *Annual Review of Anthropology*, 39, 209-223. Retrieved July 14, 2020, from www.jstor.org/stable/25735108

Svašek, M. (2007). Passions and Powers: Emotions and Globalisation. *Identities: Emotions and Globalisation*, 14(4), pp. 367-383. doi:10.1080/10702890701578415

Svašek, M. (2008). Who Cares? Families and Feelings in Movement. *Journal of Intercultural Studies: Transnational Families: Emotions and Belonging*, 29(3), pp. 213-230. doi:10.1080/07256860802169170

Svašek, M. (2012). *Moving Subjects, Moving Objects: Transnationalism, Cultural Production and Emotions*. Berghahn Books.

Svašek, M. (Ed.). (2014). *Moving Subjects, Moving Objects: Transnationalism, Cultural Production and Emotions. Affective Moves: Transit, Transition and Transformation*. Berghahn Books. Retrieved from http://www.jstor.org/stable/j.ctt9qch27

Thomas M. (2004) Losing Touch: Theorising Sensory Dislocation in the Migration Experience. Paper presented at the Migration, Affect and the Senses Conference, *Centre for Cross-Cultural Research*, Australian National University, Canberra, Australia, 16-18 June

Urry, J. (2012). *Sociology Beyond Societies: Mobilities for the Twenty-First Century*. Taylor and Francis

Urry, J. (2007). *Mobilities*. Cambridge: Polity

Vannini, P., Waskul D., Gottschalk (2012) *The senses in self, society, and culture: a sociology of the senses*.

Waite, L., Cook J., Belonging among diasporic African communities in the UK: Plurilocal homes and simultaneity of place attachments, Emotion, *Space and Society* 4 (2011) 238-248

Warin M., Dennis S., Threads of Memory: Reproducing the Cypress Tree through Sensual Consumption, *Journal of Intercultural Studies*, vol. 26, no. 1-2, 2006, pp. 159-170

Waxin, Marie-France. (2007) Chapter 12. Strategic HRM Management of International Assignments. *International Business*, Elsevier 12 : 387-438. Print

Wise, A. (2017). Transnational Affect and Emotion in Migration Research. *International Journal of Sociology*, 47(2), pp. 116-130. doi:10.1080/00207659.2017.1300468

Wise, A. (2005). Introduction: Migration, Affect and the Senses. *Journal of intercultural studies*, 26(1-2), pp. 1-3. doi:10.1080/07256860500074425

Yeoh, B. S. A., S. Huang, and T. Lam. (2005). Transnationalizing the 'Asian' family: Imaginaries, intimacies and strategic intents. *Global networks* (Oxford), 5(4), pp. 307-315. doi:10.1111/j.1471-0374.2005.00121.x

Wu, P. (2011). The impact of expatriate supporting practices and cultural intelligence on cross-cultural adjustment and performance of expatriates in Singapore. *The International Journal of Human Resource Management*, 22(13), pp. 2683-2702. doi:10.1080/09585192.2011.599956

https://nccr-onthemove.ch/.../the-mobility-of-the-highly-skilled-towards-switzerland/

https://www.pharmaceutical-technology.com/.../formula-success-inside-swiss-pharma/

https://www.swissrecruiting.com/en/personnel-recruitment-focus/life_sciences.php

https://www.aiche.org/sites/default/files/cep/20131231_2.pdf

https://www.ey.com/Publication/vwLUAssets/ey-global-mobility-cross-border-assignments-value/%24FILE/ey-HBR-Report.pdf

https://www.sem.admin.ch

Acknowledgements

This book is the culmination of a lifetime of curiosity, creativity and resilience. I would like tothank my Supervisor Dr Jacques Picard for guiding me through the intellectual gymnastics required to undertake this endeavour. I am grateful for his patience, advice, humour and encouragement. As my second Supervisor, Dr Walter Leimgruber provided me with a steady and clear focus. Thank you for always being open to dialogue and ready to exchange ideas.

My colleagues at the University of Basel, Aldina, Cedric, Christina B., Haddy, Helene, Julia B.,Katrin, Laure, Linda M., Metka & Seraina. The many discussions we have had on this topic have been invaluable. I felt welcomed and supported by each of you throughout this process.

To my students here and afar, I am one of you. You have questioned and challenged whilst I have learnt, taught and mentored you. Our interactions have been an honour and a joy; one of the many reasons why I love Academia & Anthropology.

To my parents, you embody balance & gratitude, humility & fortitude. My mother was diagnosed with Alzheimer's a year into this project and my father, as her caretaker, is the most selfless individual I know. Both have shown me the way to be in this world. Thank you.

To my informants, thank you for taking the time to share your stories, your views and comments with me.

To my three brothers, growing up with you made me fearless and courageous. I have a loud voice because of you! Thank you.

To my 3 daughters, you are my inspiration. Thank you for all the formatting, transcribing and editing. Your mother has done it!

To my husband, the wind beneath my wings, my soulmate, my champion. Thank you for reading, re-reading and being my sounding board during all this mayhem! I promise that my desk will be tidy from now on. ;)